QUEST FOR THE CELESTIAL WAND

QUEST FOR THE CELESTIAL WAND

BIANCA RODRIGUEZ JACOBS

BROWN DOG BOOKS

First published 2025

Published under licence by Brown Dog Books and
The Self-Publishing Partnership Ltd, 10b Greenway Farm,
Bath Rd, Wick, nr. Bath BS30 5RL, UK

www.selfpublishingpartnership.co.uk

ISBN printed book: 978-1-83952-878-1
ISBN e-book: 978-1-83952-879-8

Cover design by Andrew Prescott
Internal design by Andrew Easton

Printed and bound in the UK

This book is printed on FSC® certified paper

MIX
Paper | Supporting responsible forestry
FSC® C013604

For those who dare to dream.

Chapter One

Every human, whether they know it or not, has a fairy godmother to watch over and protect them. Not the kind you read about in bedtime stories, granting shallow wishes for spoilt children. But the brave and fierce kind that only appear in genuine times of need, wrapping you in warmth and banishing away darkness.

With such important duties, fairy godmothers are different to the other kinds of fairies, pixies and magical creatures you may have heard about before. They are known throughout the magical realm as the most skilled and powerful of all fairies, because of their ability to hear thoughts, grant wishes and shapeshift to walk among humans. In fact, you may have already met one without even realising. They are often nearby, showing small acts of kindness to strangers, while hiding in plain sight as they watch over you.

The stories say that fairy godmothers share a special telepathic connection with the human they care for, allowing them to sense when they are needed and communicate through their dreams. While this bond exists even for the most sceptical of humans, it is at its strongest and purest when the human believes. Indeed, in some rare cases long lost to legend, these bonds can be so strong that they have the power to break barriers between realms and channel magic for good or evil.

While to some this may all seem overly imaginative, these are all facts that stubborn twelve-year-old Darcy Holloway had always known to be true, or at least until recently, never once questioned. She had been raised to understand that real magic was all around us, if we only chose to see it. Growing up, her mother would dazzle her with the most mesmerising tales of magic and wonder, filled with accounts of brave and powerful fairies, overcoming obstacles and defeating darkness. Bedtimes were never boring. After dinner, Darcy rushed to finish her homework and brush her teeth, quick to snuggle under her duvet, eagerly awaiting the next instalment. Her mother followed happily, resting on the side of Darcy's bed, ready to share more from her endless collection of fantastic tales.

Each night, Darcy listened in awe as fairies danced through enchanted hollows and cast magic so high into the night's sky that it hit the stars with a crackle of electricity. She treasured these moments, and even as her eyelids grew heavy, she would beg her mother to keep reading while desperately trying to stay awake. Eventually and inevitably, when she had lost her fight against sleep, Darcy's mother tucked her in snugly under the covers and gave her forehead a gentle kiss. Darcy remembered those moments fondly and often. She missed her mother and wished more than anything that she could go back to those simpler times, before her mother passed away three years ago. Since then, the magic her mother once spoke about so vividly seemed harder and harder to find.

Struggling to sleep again, Darcy lay in bed restless and pulled the duvet up high around her neck. She clasped tightly onto her gemstone necklace – the last gift from her mother and the most precious thing she owned. It was a dazzling iridescent gem, slightly rough to touch and shimmering between bright turquoise and soft purple, depending on the time of day. The gem hung proudly on a gold pendant, inscribed with two dainty swans that were connected delicately by their beaks and tails, forming a small circle. Darcy's mother always told her that this symbol was an ancient fairy protection charm. As long as she was wearing the necklace, she would always be safe, and whenever she felt scared or alone, the gemstone would banish away any bad dreams.

Although Darcy no longer knew if this was true, it comforted her to think of her mother. A mixture of bittersweet happiness and yearning swelled in her chest, making her hug her precious necklace close. She tucked loose strands of her dark raven hair behind her ears and closed her eyes, hoping that her imagination alone would pull her down into a deep and peaceful dream-world slumber. Picturing exactly where she wished she could be, Darcy imagined herself dancing through the enchanted hollow from her favourite bedtime stories. Little did she know her wish would soon come true, for she was destined for an adventure even greater than she could imagine. Because if fairy godmother's have taught us anything, it's of one thing you can always be sure: even in the darkest of times, magic is never far away.

Chapter Two

As fairy tales typically lead us to believe, magic can often be found in the most unsuspecting of places. Tucked away in the rolling hills of the Wiltshire countryside, nestled within a quiet woodland clearing close to Stonehenge, hid a secret portal into a magical realm. Protected by an invisible shield, the portal was almost unnoticeable, unless recognised by the tiny markings carved into the sides of the wise old oak trees that stood guard. They were not easy to spot, always overlooked by oblivious hikers and unwitting dog walkers, simply out to enjoy the woodland. But undeniably, the tiny markings were there, if you only knew where to look. The Fairy Council liked it this way, preferring to be discreet when interfering with human business. The portal allowed them to pass freely and unnoticed into the human realm, leaving nothing more than occasional speckles of used fairy dust that fell inconspicuously into the piles of crushed, orange, autumn leaves.

On the other side of the portal was the magical realm. Although at first glance the entrance looked similar, framed by a familiar pair of mirroring oak trees surrounded by forest; it didn't take long to realise this realm was unique. After only a few steps, the woodland suddenly became denser and thicker, eventually making way for a vast clearing that surrounded a shimmering crystal lake. Everything was instantly brighter and more vivid. Colours seemed to explode to life in rich detail, yet everything felt calm as the air was filled with the melodic trills of tranquil birdsong and the soothing scents of honeysuckle, vanilla and jasmine.

To the left of the crystal lake, within a grassy meadow the colour of dazzling emeralds, stood a giant toadstool painted in bold strawberry-red with delicate marshmallow-white polka dots. The toadstool had grown many centuries ago, from the ashes of war that destroyed a magical tree that once stood in its place. Because of the magic left behind in the soil, the spectacular toadstool had the uncanny ability to produce fairy dust, the source of all fairy magic. As the centuries rolled by, the toadstool had since become the main supply of fairy dust for the realm. The fairies were grateful for this, delighted they no longer needed to travel through goblin territory to the dangerous and ancient mines to dig up crystals of fairy dust. The toadstool was therefore considered sacred and tended to with great care by groups of local fairies. They felt it was an honour, helping to preserve the beauty and resources of their natural world.

But this was not the only oddity of the magical realm. In fact, the realm was known to have many quirks and unusual features. On the other side of the enchanted clearing stood a large grassy hill stretching right up to the horizon. Overlooking the splendour of their magical toadstool and shimmering lake in the centre of their realm, this hill was home to three magical schools where each type of fairy came to learn their craft.

A tall and plump purple hawthorn tree at the base of the hill marked the entrance to Pixie Hollow, where pixies learnt the art of mischief. All around the tree, at all times of day and night, pixies could be seen whizzing through the air, testing who could fly and swerve the fastest while launching purple smoke bombs at each other to distract their competitors. If you were not careful, it was possible to end up with a face full of farting potion that would last for a week, so other fairies tended not to call there unannounced. That being said, the fun-loving pixies did know how to put on a spectacular show, and often invited the realm to regular performances of plays and poetry, which were a sure-fire way to spread cheer through the land.

Progressing further up the hill led to the middle of the three schools. Hidden behind a set of large cream-coloured, bone-textured gates covered in tiny pearl teeth was a dramatic-looking castle where studious young tooth fairies learnt their trade. Tooth fairies were considered to be highly smart and skilled fairies, having to pass at least three exams before graduation. This included a notoriously difficult 'sneaking test' where fairies competed to discreetly replace a tooth that had been hidden under a pillow, with the largest possible stack of gold coins, all without waking a sleeping human. It was only then that they were considered ready to enter the human realm and were granted fairy dust to travel through the magical portal unsupervised.

Attendance at the highest school on the hill was a matter of prestige for fairy families across the realm, all of them hoping their young fairies would be deemed worthy of becoming fairy godmothers. This was considered the greatest privilege, making them responsible for protecting a human and helping their human to achieve their wildest dreams. Sitting proudly on the summit was this most coveted of all fairy schools, The Hummingbird Academy for Fairy Godmothers.

Founded many thousands of moons ago, The Hummingbird Academy for Fairy Godmothers was renowned throughout all magical kingdoms. Its mirrored castle-like structure reached high towards the skyline, dominating the surrounding landscape with a sharp central spire, decorated with lavish engravings and multi-coloured crystals representing each of the magical elemental forces. Each individual engraving had once been delicately etched into the glass tower by every fairy godmother who had passed through the academy, leaving behind a small signature as part of their graduation ceremony. The overall effect was spectacular to see, a combination of beauty and strength, and a reminder to the realm of the collective power of fairies who work together for the forces of good.

Each year on the harvest moon, the academy welcomed new fairies from around the world who also dreamt of carving their own name into the crystal tower one day and becoming fully fledged fairy godmothers. As the sun slowly set over the horizon, shimmering flecks of gold, orange and pink danced over the academy, acting as a glowing beacon for the imminent arrivals as they climbed the hill with anticipation.

Packed in like sardines, these aspiring first years gathered in the cathedral-like Great Hall. They were easily spotted with their white tunics and excited, often apprehensive expressions. The hall was alive with activity. Chatter echoed around the room, bouncing off the grand marble columns and high arched ceilings. In every direction, new students gathered, dodging piles of magical floating luggage and trying to find their new dormitory mates.

In the middle of the crowd, a slightly nervous Elendil stood with his proud elder sister, Marta. Just like Marta, Elendil had striking blond hair and bright blue eyes that were framed by thin-rimmed glasses. The slight point to their ears and slanted cheeks were a nod to their half-elf, half-fairy heritage; something that until a few centuries ago, would not have been accepted within the academy. Marta stood alongside Eli in a deep pink tunic and cloak. Unlike new starters at the academy, more experienced fairies wore uniforms in colours of every shade. These colours represented their personalities and Marta explained to Eli that his colour would soon be revealed as part of their initiation ceremony.

'Are you sure you have everything, Eli?' asked Marta.

'Yeah, I think so, sis. I've definitely got all my books and I can't wait to check out the enchanted library later,' Eli replied.

She teased back, 'I know you like to study, Eli, but remember that nerds can have fun too! I can't carry the burden of being the most interesting sibling forever, you know.' As Marta giggled, she was startled by a loud thump. Eli staggered forwards as a dark, tall and broad fairy bumped into him.

'Sorry, mate, I can barely see over this pile of luggage. Are you okay?' asked the apologetic-looking fairy staring back at Eli. 'Sorry, how rude of me, I'm Felix Thunderbolt.'

Eli laughed. 'To be honest, I suppose I should actually thank you for interrupting my sister Marta fussing over me. I'm Elendil Evenstar, Eli for short. Nice to meet you, Felix.'

Marta pretended to look less than impressed, peering over her glasses at her juvenile younger brother. 'Look, I may be slightly overbearing, but I do mean well!' countered Marta. 'Nice to meet you too, Felix. Is that "Thunderbolt", as in from the famous Thunderbolt family? Sorry to pry, I'm just a bit nosey like that.'

Felix ran his hands through his short, thick hair; a blend of tight black curls punctuated by a sharp streak of silver down the middle, as if to make his surname more obvious. Something that looked like embarrassment sat behind his bright green eyes as he answered Marta. 'Yeah, that's me. But being a descendant of a long line of realm-renowned dream casters can be a lot to live up to. At times it just feels a bit daunting,' he added candidly.

In that moment, Eli noticed two other fairies in white tunics glaring over at him. Scarlett Frost and Stella Skyswan sauntered over, tutting as they walked past and talking just loud enough to be overheard. 'Urgh, I guess they're letting anyone in nowadays,' huffed Scarlett, a tall silver-blonde fairy who carried herself like she thought she was better than everyone else. Scarlett came from a powerful and respected fairy family. While that meant she was privileged in many ways, unfortunately she was also short on manners. Scarlett's best friend Stella, a shorter fairy with cropped light blue hair, was equally dismissive as she scoffed, 'I know, what a disgrace. Now they've let the elves in, it'll be goblins before we know it.'

Eli stared down at the ground not knowing how to respond. He scuffed his boots against the marble floor feeling ashamed. Marta was ever the protective sister. She hugged him tightly and told him not to worry. 'Remember, take no notice of those nasty fairies, they're so stuck up they can't even tell what phase of the moon we're in.'

Marta had also grown used to similar remarks ever since she first decided she wanted to be a fairy godmother. Since then, she had worked harder than any of her peers, always seeking to prove herself and showing great determination. As a result of this, she had excelled in her first year at the academy, finishing top of most of her classes. She hoped to perform just as well in her second year at the academy, and knew her smart little brother Eli could achieve the same too.

As Marta hugged Eli, Felix noticed he had dropped his dormitory assignment card on the floor. He bent down to pick it up but was beaten to it by another fairy dressed in white, with olive skin, purple irises and autumnal-red hair. He couldn't help but stare. She was one of the most beautiful fairies he'd ever seen.

'Here you go,' said the red-haired fairy handing back the card. 'I'm Bella Brightheart, by the way,' she added with a confident grin.

'Very kind of you,' replied a slightly bemused Felix. He was clearly not used to being slower than other fairies given his athletic build and seemed to be just as competitive as Bella. Eli and Marta chuckled lightly and introduced themselves.

Bella smiled. 'I'm looking for my dorm mates. Do any of you happen to know where Kingfisher Hall is?'

Marta clapped gleefully and pulled Bella into a warm hug. 'No way!' she exclaimed excitedly. 'You're in Kingfisher too! That's brilliant news! I was worried I was just going to be stuck with these gross boys all year.'

They all laughed, instantly feeling less nervous about their own worries for the year ahead knowing that they had each other to lean on. It was a wholesome moment that Marta was first to interrupt. 'Now that you've made some friends, Eli, I'll leave you all to it. I've got to go and join the choir up front so Principal Featherstone can start your induction ceremony. Have fun all of you.' With that, Marta hurried off to the opulent stage that had been set up at the front of the hall.

The orchestra sat poised and patient already on stage next to the choir. Being part of the orchestra or choir was a highly sought-after role that was obtained by invitation only, and only for the most musically talented fairies in all the academy. Although even first years could join, this was typically rare. They were led at the front by a conductor dressed smartly for the occasion in dark purple robes, with a matching butterfly bow tie. As the conductor lifted his wand to start playing, the orchestra responded with heavenly notes from their crystal instruments, introducing the choir's angelic rendition of the Hummingbird Academy's anthem, 'Two Worlds, One Earth, One Hope'.

Chapter Three

As the song came to an end, the Great Hall fell silent for all but a beat, before a spontaneous eruption of applause, cheering and raucous whistling from the audience. After all, fairies do know how to celebrate. Delighted with a wonderful performance, the conductor took a small bow and lowered his wand, signalling to the orchestra that they could leave the stage. The brightly dressed choir followed suit, equally satisfied with a job well done. Marta hurried back to Eli's side, joining her first-year dormitory mates for their head mistress' welcome speech and initiation ceremony.

As the stage cleared, the signature sound of Principal Featherstone's sharp stilettos clicked across the marble floor, growing in intensity as she emerged from the crowd and approached the stage. She wore a deep orange cloak that matched her irises and enhanced the shimmer of her almost translucent silvery skin. Her hair was known to change colour with her emotions, which today meant her candy-floss pink curls were piled high into a loose bun on top of her head. While she looked whimsical, there was no doubt she was also fierce. She took great pride in her role at the academy and that was evident as soon as she started speaking.

'Good evening, everyone. Happy Harvest Moon to you all and a very warm welcome to our new first-year fairy godmothers. For those who don't know me, I am Loretta Featherstone, your head mistress here at the Hummingbird Academy. I have been in this role for over one hundred and twenty years and it remains my pleasure to guide you on your magical journey of discovery to becoming fairy godmothers. Before we begin our ceremony this evening, I'd like to start by thanking Professor Avery Curtis, our impeccable conductor and choir master, for what I'm sure you'll all agree was a delightful performance.' Further cheers came from the crowd, prompting Professor Curtis to stand for another, this time more flamboyant bow.

When the cheers had quietened, the head mistress continued, 'As some of you will know, Professor Curtis is not only a wonderful musician, but also a very talented dream caster, who will guide our students in the art of dream manipulation, a key magical tool we use to help our human connections and hear their thoughts. He has a long record of training some of the most renowned dream casters, including several Thunderbolts, so rest assured, you are all in very safe wings.'

Hearing the mention of Felix's famous family, Eli smiled over at him, while Bella gave him a gentle nudge and conspiratorial wink, making him chuckle.

'It is also my pleasure to introduce Professor Melody Fairweather, our resident realm jumping and shape shifting instructor. Professor Fairweather is highly experienced, having spent over a hundred years working as a fairy godmother, travelling to the human realm and beyond. I can honestly say that what this fairy doesn't know about fairy dust, really isn't worth knowing,' teased Principal Featherstone, clearly finding her flow. Professor Fairweather stood up and gave a small twirl, showing off her beautifully patterned turquoise gown and chunky beaded crystal jewellery. Her precisely plaited hair framed her dark complexion and bright white irises. She looked equal parts friendly and formidable, just as Bella had imagined.

Loretta Featherstone continued, 'Finally, please allow me to introduce Professor Evangeline Joy, master wish wielder and expert in conjuring and spells. In due time, you will all get the privilege of learning from Professor Joy, but as you will likely know, wish wielding is considered the most dangerous of all fairy godmother skills, so it does not form part of your curriculum until second year, when you have mastered the basics of fairy godmother training. This is also when you will receive your first wands.'

Professor Joy sprung to her feet giving a gentle wave to the crowd. She was a vision in deep emerald green, with a bright blonde bob that framed her sea-blue eyes and delicate features. She was such a poised and dainty-looking fairy that it was hard to believe she was a wish wielder; yet the rows of trophies floating proudly in her office proved she was both feisty and formidable.

As the introductions finished, anticipation buzzed through the congregation of new fairies dressed in white and clustered in the middle of the hall. They knew they would shortly be invited to complete the initiation ceremony and finally discover the colour of their magic. It was one of the highlights of being at the academy and something every former student remembered fondly when starting their careers.

'Good luck, Eli,' whispered Marta, giving him a nudge.

'Good luck, everyone,' Eli, Bella and Felix repeated to each other in unison.

Brimming with pride, Principal Featherstone continued her speech. 'It is now my honour to invite you all to pledge yourselves to helping humanity, protecting the secret of our existence and using your powers for the forces of good. When you are ready, please each take a handful of fairy dust from the bowl that Professor Fairweather is bringing round.'

Melody Fairweather circled the room, mingling with her new students. She carried an ornate ivory bowl that was piled high with a seemingly endless supply of glittering magical dust. It shimmered when kissed by the moonlight streaming in through the stained-glass windows around the edge of the hall. Hoping to calm any nerves, she smiled warmly at every new student as they each took a generous handful from the bowl.

'On my count, throw the fairy dust high into the air above you and chant along with me: Two worlds, One Earth, One Hope,' Principal Featherstone added dramatically.

As instructed, the students launched their fairy dust high into the air above them. It floated there for a moment, suspended as a collective cloud of glitter above their heads, twinkling with every colour of the rainbow. The crowd chanted, creating a harmonious hum that caused the glittering cloud to vibrate as if itself was undecided how long it would hang suspended in space. The magic smelt like cinnamon, comforting and warm. After a few seconds more, the cloud collapsed downward, drenching the students in thick sparkling dust. As it settled, the fairy dust dissolved, melting delicately into their robes like the first snowflakes of winter and causing each previously white tunic to change before their eyes until the hall was an explosion of colour.

Bella Brightheart gasped excitedly as her robes became a rich burgundy, matching her hair and determined personality. By her side, Felix Thunderbolt watched in awe as his cloak turned green, while Eli's tunic changed to a bright royal blue.

'Isn't this amazing?' shouted Bella.

'Incredible,' agreed Eli, bringing a tear of pride to Marta's eyes.

Felix clapped in excitement. 'This is just the beginning! Just wait until classes start tomorrow and we actually get to use our magic!'

All around them, the room danced with colours of all shades and tones. To their left, a tall fairy called Finn Breezecharm was now dressed in a light icy blue. He was chatting animatedly to Tempest and Talia Summersong, affectionately known as 'the twins'. The Summersong twins were never far apart and could often be seen together sitting in silence, preferring to use their telepathic twin connection to gossip in private. They were almost identical in looks, with pretty long auburn hair and hazel eyes, but had vastly different personalities. Tempest, the louder twin, proudly paraded her new olive-green ensemble, while Talia smiled and gently smoothed down her dress, pleased it was now her favourite shade of lilac.

Across the room, Scarlett Frost twirled in her vibrant red cloak, showing off to Stella who now wore a deep inky blue. As Scarlett twirled, she tactfully bumped into Gale Storm, successfully stealing the heartthrob's attention from his reflection in the stained-glass window. Gale was a handsome first-year student dressed in deep grey. He had dreams of becoming a professional wish wielder after graduating and was blessed with athleticism to match, which was lucky because he wasn't known to be 'the brightest firefly in the jar'. He stood next to his best friend Jupiter Riversage, calm, studious and dressed in mustard yellow.

With all the excitement in the hall, Principal Featherstone held her wand to her throat, using it to amplify her voice and regain the crowd's attention. 'Congratulations, everyone, on gaining your colours and starting the most wonderful journey to becoming fairy godmothers. You have pledged yourselves to protecting humanity and keeping our worlds in balance, and for that I am truly grateful. As fairies, you are blessed with incredible power, the likes of which you have never known and will spend your time here trying to understand and control. While your paths will undoubtedly have their challenges, I know you will rise above them together and make us all proud. I wish you every success here. I wish you peace. And above all, I wish that you make bonds of life-long friendship. Your lessons will start tomorrow, but for now relax, get to know your fellow fairies and most importantly, enjoy the party.' She then gave a swift nod to Professor Curtis, who, understanding his cue, re-started the band.

Within moments, the Great Hall was once again alive with music and sounds of merriment. The musical taste of fairies was known to be eclectic, switching with each song from jazz and swing, to dance, trance and rock and roll. Professor Curtis dutifully took requests at the front of the hall, clearly in his element. He led the band masterfully, conducting them from a heavy, old and slightly tattered blue leather-bound book that seemingly contained a near-endless supply of sheet music.

As another staple of any good fairy festival, the refreshments were also free-flowing. At the edge of the hall, huge fountains of sweet amber-coloured nectar fizz appeared, alongside giant hive-shaped honey cakes and tall trees with blossoms of blue and pink candy floss. Marta grabbed Bella, excitedly dragging her over to the nectar fountain and filling a tulip cup to the brim for her to try. Felix and Eli rushed to the trees, plucking off great handfuls of candy floss and gobbling them greedily. After the excitement of the earlier ceremony, the students enjoyed the chance to relax, dancing and feasting in collective harmony, excited for more magic to come.

Chapter Four

After a long evening of partying, the friends returned to their dorm room in Kingfisher Hall with heavy feet and wide smiles. Although fairies were well known for their decadent and long-running parties, this event had felt particularly indulgent. Feeling the after-effects of all the dancing and sugary treats, the friends each collapsed in a heap on their plush four-poster beds, tired and happy. They had all expected it to be a brilliant introduction to life at the academy, and they had not been disappointed.

'Wasn't that such a wonderful evening?' squealed Marta, propping herself up onto her elbows ready to gossip. 'You boys ate so much candy floss, I thought you hadn't eaten for a week.'

'To be fair, Marta, I think we almost drained the fountain of nectar fizz,' teased Bella, kicking off her chunky boots. 'But it was brilliant fun and nice to get to know some of our new classmates too. The twins seem cool, albeit a bit whacky, even by fairy godmother standards.'

Eli nodded in agreement. 'Finn seems like a nice guy too. Did you know he also collects unusual objects? I can't wait to show him my collections of buttons and paperclips.'

Marta chuckled and rolled her eyes. 'Oh little brother, you can be such a geek sometimes.'

Felix sat down next to Eli on the side of his bed and gave him a gentle teasing nudge with his elbow. 'Yeah, who knew elves could be so much fun?'

Eli responded with lightning quick humour, 'Well, who knew fairies could have such questionable dancing?'

Felix feigned insult and got to his feet with a shimmy. 'You mean you don't like these wild moves?' Taking centre stage on the rug between their beds, Felix attempted an odd routine across the floor that resembled something like break-dancing mixed with a moonwalk. The floorboards creaked loudly in complaint and the friends fell about laughing, collapsing back onto their beds.

'I can't believe we're finally here,' Eli sighed wistfully in a moment of blissful disbelief prompting them all to reflect on their new surroundings. Kingfisher Hall was a grand building, carved from ancient stone that seemed as old as the realm itself. The dormitory had been there since the academy first opened many centuries ago and it was a firm favourite for fairy godmothers given its long heritage, wonderful views and, in true fairy fashion, its proximity to the nearby pantry. Its high ceilings made way for a large arched window in the centre of the room where purple moonlight streamed in, casting shadows across the centre of the floor. Looking out of the grand window gave a breathtaking view of the shimmering lake and on a clear night, even the magical toadstool could be seen far in the distance, lit by the canopy of stars overhead.

As the moonlight danced around the room, the friends were able to catch a better glimpse of the ornate patterns around the walls and ceiling. Upon inspection, it was clear that these markings were engravings from past students. It looked like a glorious collage. Bella suspected it was them practising how they would sign their name into the main tower when they graduated. It had become somewhat of a tradition in the academy and something that the friends dreamt of doing themselves one day when they had completed their third and final year of study. The inscriptions formed a beautiful pattern that covered the ceiling and extended all the way down most of the walls, like an intricate tattoo that grew sparser towards the floor.

Felix had never seen something so beautiful. Sure, he'd heard lots of stories from his family over the years about what the academy was like, but being here was something altogether different. His parents had met at the academy and fallen in love, going on to create a large brood that they were very proud of. Felix's four brothers and one sister had all attended the academy before him, recounting endless tales of how much they had enjoyed their time here, before going on to achieve incredible feats of dream casting and cementing the powerful Thunderbolt name across the realm. Growing up as the youngest of six siblings, Felix had always been considered the baby of the family and felt under pressure to live up to his family's high standards. This was a burden he was now keen to shake off, eager to prove himself and make his own mark on the world. He propped himself up on his bed, admiring the room around him.

The dormitory itself was not just beautifully decorated, but also well equipped. In each corner of the room stood a large mahogany bed decorated in the newly awarded colours of each of the fairies, clearly signposting where each of them would sleep. Next to each bed was a small table adorned with a crystal lamp, alongside a spacious wardrobe and desk.

'It really is beautiful in here,' stated Bella. 'But where's all our stuff?'

She jumped off her bed and flung open her wardrobe to investigate, gasping in surprise to find all her belongings neatly folded and arranged.

'One of the perks of attending a magical school,' laughed Marta. 'Everything is already unpacked.' She continued, 'I don't expect your stuff will stay that neat for long though, Eli.'

Eli rolled his eyes. 'I'm not THAT messy, sis. Besides, at least I don't leave hedgehog food lying around everywhere.'

'You know Luna likes to snack, Eli,' tutted Marta in his direction. 'She needs to eat a lot before she goes into hibernation,' she clarified.

'Wait. Are you saying you have a pet hedgehog?' asked Felix.

Marta nodded. 'Just wait till you meet her. She's awesome.'

Felix looked puzzled. 'I can't imagine having a pet hedgehog. Don't they just end up stabbing you quite a lot?'

'No, she's a sweetheart really. It's only when she's grumpy or scared that you need to be extra careful, because then she has a habit of disappearing,' advised Marta.

'That's understandable,' agreed Felix. 'Sometimes I want to run away from it all too.'

'Yeah, but when I say "disappearing", I do mean literally. She has a bizarre talent of being able to become invisible,' explained Marta.

'Wow! A magical hedgehog!' exclaimed Bella, another animal lover. 'That almost makes my pet seem dull,' she laughed. 'I've brought along Dorothy, my giant African land snail.'

'I'm sure they'll be best friends, just like us,' said Marta, with a wink.

As if perfectly on cue, the friends jumped to a knock at the door. A tall blond fairy who was dressed in yellow and looked a few years older than them wheeled in a small golden cart. He looked friendly, and also vaguely familiar, although the friends couldn't figure out why.

'Sorry for the delay getting these to you,' he smiled. 'They've both been fed and watered and I'm sure they're excited to see you again.' The fairy carefully carried a gold-edged cage over to Marta's desk and placed it down gently. Inside was a small furry-looking hedgehog, curled up in a ball, snoring peacefully. Much to Felix's surprise, the hedgehog actually looked quite sweet and cuddly, not that he'd care to admit that. He'd never had much time for pets, but that was probably understandable given his upbringing in such a loud and full household.

'For something named after the moon, she sure does like to sleep,' laughed Eli.

On the other side of the room, the blond fairy in the yellow cloak took another cage over to Bella's desk. Inside,

Dorothy the giant snail was perched happily on a little log, munching away on half a cucumber. 'It's good to see you, girl,' Bella whispered lovingly to the cage. She'd had Dorothy since she was a young fairy and she had since become a trusted confidante. It all started when Bella was old enough to feel disappointed at being an only child and had relentlessly begged her parents for a sibling, or a pet. Eventually, her parents conceded, agreeing to buy her a pet without fur. They'd settled on a giant African land snail and the pair had been inseparable ever since.

Once the pets were both settled in, Bella and Marta thanked the tall fairy for bringing them along. 'It's my pleasure,' he said, introducing himself as Neptune Summersong, the twins' older brother. 'I work down in our animal and nature house, looking after our grounds and animals here, so please do stop by for a visit if you ever fancy it.'

Marta blushed. 'That's lovely. Thanks, Neptune. Hopefully see you around.' Neptune smiled back. It looked like he wanted to say something else but thought better of it and retreated. He steered the trolley back out of the room and closed the door gently behind him.

Bella giggled, throwing a pillow over at Marta. 'He clearly fancies you,' she laughed.

'He does seem rather sweet,' conceded Marta. 'But we're here to study, so let's focus on that, shall we?'

The group's attention quickly returned to their lessons that would be starting tomorrow. 'We're going to be learning how to realm jump tomorrow. Can you believe it?' Felix sounded excited.

'And then it'll be dream casting,' added Eli, glancing playfully back at Felix, 'and because we're not all famous Thunderbolts like you, I'd really like to get a head start on learning the basics. Anyone fancy a trip to the library tonight?'

'The library? Tonight?' questioned Felix. 'We haven't even started lessons yet, Eli.'

Marta rolled her eyes knowingly. 'That's my geeky brother for you.' She laughed and turned to Eli. 'You'll probably have to sneak into "the enchanted section" for dream casting books. They're not considered "standard fairy myths and magic", so they're probably kept out of the main library.'

Eli looked worried. He was usually very obedient and didn't like breaking rules or the thought of sneaking in somewhere he wasn't supposed to be. Bella sensed his concerns and while she wasn't usually much of a bookworm, she didn't mind a bit of mischief and was always up for helping a friend in need. She turned to Eli. 'I'll come with you, Eli, and I've got an idea to sneak us in.' Turning to Marta with a mischievous twinkle in her eye, she added, 'Marta, please could I borrow Luna?'

Chapter Five

With Luna the hedgehog snuggled up safely in Bella's pocket, Bella and Eli hurried down the corridors leading to the library, while trying to remain as quiet as possible. Kingfisher Hall was connected to the main academy through a network of underground tunnels that zigzagged erratically, as if at their own discretion. Cold, gloomy and lit only by enchanted candlelight, the tunnels meandered mysteriously, making it easy to get lost as each passageway separated off like arteries towards different parts of the building. It was unclear how these tunnels all connected together. There had been several official attempts to document the pathways over the years, with the hope of finally creating an accurate map. But each of these attempts had ended in failure, some even with disastrous or deadly consequences. The fairies suspected this was because the tunnels really did have a mind of their own and were quite happy to pick and choose who they helped and who they hindered. It was said that this network of passageways existed even before the academy was formally founded; back in the ancient era of the realm that was filled with so much conflict that it still haunted the bedtime stories of young fairies today. During this dark period, the corridors were used to smuggle fairy dust from faraway magic mines to be used in the battle against power-thirsty goblins who were trying to dominate the realm. The tunnels varied in size and shape, with uneven concrete floor tiles that sloped randomly as if to defy logic. They were cavernous, echoey and notoriously hard to navigate, which made them the perfect hiding place for all sorts of magical objects and enchantments, some of which had never again been found.

Dampness and intrigue seemed to linger in the tunnels, making Bella and Eli shiver. While they couldn't be totally sure of their direction, lopsided signposts seemed to appear from thin air at each junction, letting them know they were on the right path to their destination. Eventually, after what felt like hours, Bella and Eli saw a faint glow up ahead in the distance. As they walked closer, the tunnel closed in around them to a small archway. A slightly wonky sign swung over an old wooden door, indicating they had reached the library.

Nervously, Eli pushed open the creaky old door in front of them, unsure what to expect on the other side. Relief flooded through him as they were instantly greeted by the comforting smell of old books stacked high on shelves up to the ceiling, stretching on for rows and rows in either direction. At the far end of the room, Bella and Eli could see a cosy lounge complete with two plush leather sofas centred in front of a gently smouldering fire. Beyond this was a row of unoccupied desks with large green glass lamps, creating the perfect space for students to study. Although they expected these desks were usually full of studious fairies, fortunately they were currently empty, with everyone else merrily exhausted after the party. The sight excited Eli, who had always loved learning new things. He could already picture himself spending hours on end here, cosied up with a text book or two, trying to perfect his craft. Bella, on the other hand, had never been one to enjoy studying. She was very practical and would much rather have practised her skills in real life, learning through trial and error, instead of reading about them first.

Bella and Eli continued to scan the room. Marta had warned the pair that they would need to look for 'the enchanted section'. Surely it couldn't be too hard to find, Bella thought while looking around the vast space. She had expected to see something obvious. Another sign perhaps, or a shimmering archway. But as with the best fairy enchantments, magic is often hidden in plain sight.

'The entrance has to be around here somewhere,' pondered Bella.

Eli looked equally puzzled. 'You're right. We must be missing something.'

The library was deserted at this hour, so the pair wondered over to the comfy sofas to warm up by the fire and think. They sank down into the plush padding and leant towards the fire, seeking to warm their hands after their trip through the cold, dank tunnels.

'Do you feel that?' Bella asked Eli, noticing something strange.

'No, what?' he responded.

'That's exactly what I mean,' she replied, as if a light bulb turned on in her mind, 'there's no heat coming from that fire.'

Eli leant in closer to feel what she meant. The fire was a perfect illusion. 'It must be the same kind of magic used to disguise the portal to the human realm.'

Bella agreed. 'It seems like the perfect place to hide a secret section of the library if you ask me. I reckon it's a portal. Shall we try and jump through?'

Barely finishing her sentence and intrigued by the thought of adventure, Bella strode over to the fireplace and turned back to offer an outstretched hand to Eli. He wouldn't normally have tried something so brazen, instead probably opting to head back to the dormitory empty handed. But although he was anxious about heading through the portal into the unknown, something about Bella made Eli feel calm. He got up from the sofa and took her hand.

'On the count of three, we jump,' said Bella authoritatively. Eli took a deep breath and nodded.

'One… two… three…' they counted slowly in unison, before leaping forward through the fake flames in front of them.

Half expecting to be scalded from the fire, Eli and Bella landed through the portal with a dull thud onto a dusty rust-coloured rug. They glanced behind them to see a mirror image of the fire illusion from the other side of the fireplace. They breathed a sigh of relief. It confirmed the portal was still open and they would be able to get back through when they had completed their secret mission. For now, they remained hidden behind a sofa similar to the one they had been sitting on moments before.

'Hopefully we'll get better at the landing part once we start lessons,' Bella whispered to Eli. 'Are you okay?'

'Yeah, all good! That was actually easier than I expected,' Eli whispered back, surprising himself slightly at how much he enjoyed doing something so spontaneous.

Bella smiled. 'Well, that's step one done at least. Now for step two of the plan – getting you into the enchanted section.'

They peaked out from behind the sofa, cautiously glancing around the room to get a sense of their new surroundings. This room was much smaller than the one they had come from, which made it feel warmer and more inviting. In the far corner, was a large curved desk made of smooth patterned marble. On top sat a bronze typewriter, alongside a beautiful bouquet of cream lilies and lilac wildflowers that spilled over the edge of an elaborate crystal vase like a waterfall. Curiously, behind the elegant desk was a silver door that seemed to be softly glowing, in the otherwise dimly lit room.

'That must be the enchanted section,' guessed Eli, fuelled by adrenalin. 'It's the only way out of this room.'

Bella agreed. 'It looks like this is some kind of waiting area. We're lucky we haven't been caught by the receptionist.'

With that, just as if they were jinxed, Bella and Eli heard soft footsteps approaching from the distance. From their safe hiding place behind the sofa, they could see the shadow of a fairy taking a seat behind the desk. The silent room was then suddenly filled with the sound of determined typing and absentminded humming.

'This just got a bit more complicated.' Bella frowned and thought for a moment. 'Change of plan, Eli. Luna and I will have to create a distraction so you can sneak in round the back. I'll meet you in there, we grab the book and we get out. Got it?'

Eli grimaced. He didn't like the sound of going in alone, but had come too far to back out now. Bella sensed his reluctance. 'You can do this, Eli. We'll be back in the dorm room laughing about this with the others in no time, I promise,' she encouraged. 'Ready?'

'Okay, let's do this,' Eli whispered in confirmation. If he had already done one thing this evening that made him nervous, he knew he could find the confidence to do one more.

Before Eli could back out, Bella crawled out quietly from behind the sofa. She approached the desk timidly, conveniently taking note of the name card beside the bouquet of flowers. She was used to being mischievous and knew exactly how to get what she wanted. This would be simple enough.

'Mrs Nightingale?' She continued sweetly, 'I'm really sorry to bother you. I've lost my pet hedgehog, Luna, and I'm really worried about her. I think she ran through in here somewhere. Do you think you could help me find her?'

Belinda Nightingale peered curiously over the top of her thin spectacles to see Bella. She was a jolly-looking fairy, dressed in bright teal that contrasted against her rosy cheeks, silver hair and golden eyes. After deeming Bella authentic, she smiled and replied kindly, 'Well of course, my dear, it would be my pleasure. We can't have a little lost hedgehog running around now, can we?'

As she got to her feet to step out from behind the desk, Eli, who had now snuck to the other side of the sofa, saw his chance to move. He quickly dashed to hide behind a nearby marble pillar, ready to make his escape. As Bella started an award-worthy performance of leading Mrs Nightingale on a wild hedgehog chase around the room, he slipped out of view discreetly through the mysterious silver door.

Chapter Six

When Eli pushed through the silver door, there was no doubt in his mind that he was now in the enchanted section of the library. He found himself in a large domed room, framed with huge old-fashioned wooden bookshelves and sliding ladders as tall as trees. Moonlight streamed in through a large skylight overhead, bathing the room in silver light, making it feel bright and mysterious. The walls below were decorated in gold leaf with patterns of all the known constellations.

Eli wandered closer to the bookshelves, hoping to find the dream casting section. As he got closer, he could see how beautiful the bookshelves were, made of cherrywood with detailed carvings of some of fairy folks' favourite flowers. Huge roses stretched across the room twisting along prickly vines, while foxgloves and honeysuckle climbed high towards the moonlight. As Eli admired the delicate craftsmanship, a glimmer of light by his side caught his eye. Along the wall closest to him he noticed a message appearing, letter by letter, as if the air itself was becoming ink. The text shimmered as he glanced at it, but no sooner than it appeared, it seemed to vanish once again. Eli had read about mysterious vanishing ink like this and suspected it was a 'hidden truth' enchantment, used to send secret messages to particular fairies, only revealing itself when the reader was deemed worthy. He glanced at the wall again, elated to catch a glimpse of the message: *Dream of what you seek to find; it hides much deeper in your mind. If enchantment is what you seek; your truth, you only need to speak.*

As with many fairy enchantments, and not for the first time today, Eli knew the answer to this magical riddle was likely to be hidden in plain sight. He decided to try taking the text literally and spoke truthfully towards the secret message on the wall. 'I am Elendil Evenstar and I would like to learn how to dream cast.' Eli added politely, 'Please.'

For a moment, there was only stillness and silence. Eli frowned, disappointed that speaking his truth hadn't seemed to achieve anything. He really thought he'd understood the message and reluctantly headed back towards the bookshelf, contemplating how long it would take him to find what he was looking for manually in the huge room of books. As he thought about climbing one of the ladders, he heard a rustle from one of the nearby rows high above him. Eli turned towards the noise. Alarmingly, he could see several of the books now shaking; vibrating against each other as if they wanted to escape. The hum of vibrating books grew louder and louder until a large volume in the middle started to wriggle forwards, as if trying to free itself. It kept wobbling until it finally reached the edge of the shelf, toppling dramatically spine first towards the ground. As the book began to fall, its covers spread wide open causing its pages to flutter miraculously, just like butterfly wings. Avoiding a catastrophic fall, the book floated gracefully towards Eli, pirouetting a few times as if to show off before landing softly in his hands. Speechless, Eli admired the book in front of him. It was thick and heavy, with a navy blue hardback leather cover and an unusual gold marking on the spine that looked like two swans forming a circle. It was both peculiar and magical. Eli had never seen anything like it.

Eli had always been considered to be geeky by his older sister, Marta, and she had always teased him about it. In truth, he'd never minded. He knew he was intelligent and loved to learn new things, absorbing the world around him like a great sponge. Being in the enchanted section was no exception. He was itching with excitement, eager to open the book and find out what secrets were hidden inside. But no sooner had he lifted the front cover than he was suddenly alerted by quiet footsteps approaching from behind, causing him to freeze.

'Psst, Eli, it's me,' whispered Bella.

'Phew,' exhaled Eli. 'How did you get away from Mrs Nightingale?'

'It was easy really. Once I thought you'd taken long enough to get the book, I took Luna out of my pocket and pretended to find her. Then Mrs Nightingale went to get us a cup of honeydew tea and I snuck through to find you while she was gone.' Bella smiled smugly. She had always been good at thinking on her feet and she'd even impressed herself with her cunningness this time.

'You're a genius, Bella!' Eli smiled in return.

'Sometimes I think I might be half pixie. My parents certainly tell me that.' Bella giggled and spent a moment looking round at the enchanted library in front of her. 'It's pretty cool in here, I can see why you wanted to visit.'

She glanced round the room admiring the beautiful bookshelves, when her eyes strayed towards a strange warm light flickering dimly from a doorway in the corner.

'What's that over there?' she asked Eli curiously. 'It looks like it might be another room?'

Eli was completely confused. 'I've got no idea. It definitely wasn't here before you arrived.'

Feeling baffled but brave, Bella began to walk slowly towards the flickering light, trying to keep as quiet as possible. She snuck across the floorboards, gesturing for Eli to follow. As they approached the doorway, they could see the soft glow of enchanted candlelight spilling out through the slightly open door. Bella and Eli kept hidden, trying to make out the hushed and anxious sounding voices coming from inside.

Through the thin crack, Bella and Eli could just about make out the shadows of several figures inside the adjacent room, gathered around a large marble oval table. Illuminated by enchanted candlelight, it was easy to recognise their principal, Loretta Featherstone, alongside teachers from their initiation ceremony. In a dramatically different look for Loretta, her colour-changing hair hung in tight red curls over her orange cloak, mirroring her grave expression. By her side, usually cheerful Professor Evangeline Joy and Professor Melody Fairweather looked equally serious. They were flanked by the deep purple robe of an equally sombre-looking Professor Avery Curtis. The mood in the room felt tense to say the least. Bella and

Eli squirmed awkwardly. They knew they shouldn't be witnessing this secret gathering, despite stumbling on it accidentally, and they certainly knew they shouldn't stay to listen. For a brief moment they considered walking away, but something stopped them in their tracks. They just couldn't bring themselves to leave.

Bella and Eli squinted through the doorway, trying to make out the faces of the four other fairies sat round the far side of the table. Next to Professor Curtis was a tall male figure, with silver eyes and long white hair that made him seem old and wise. He wore an elaborate grey cloak, detailed with silver symbols that looked reminiscent of fairy signs. However, it was the slant to his cheeks and point-tipped ears that gave away his true identity as Aelfric Albion, Elder of the Elves.

To his side was a curious-looking fairy, wrapped up like a present in a silver crinkly foil-like dress. She looked smart and serious, with bright green eyes, auburn hair and a slight pout to her expression. Bella admired the dainty pearl chain that hung round her neck, until noticing on closer inspection that the delicate misshapen pearls were actually a string of small milk teeth.

'That must be Morgan Ivory, Chief of the Tooth Fairies,' Bella whispered to Eli.

He nodded and whispered back, 'And the one sat next to her with the dark hair must be Eden Briar. She's the leader of the pixies. That must make this a meeting of the Fairy Council.' The pair shuddered at the realisation.

Eden Briar looked serious and stylish in a somehow fashionable green-and-pink ruffled dress, but she was still not the most striking guest in the room. At the head of the table sat the most regal fairy that Bella and Eli had ever seen. Dressed in drapes of sugared-lilac satin and velvet, with incredible purple-blue iridescent jewellery and a magnificent crown of golden flowers, it was quite apparent that Bella and Eli were in the presence of royalty. The queen of the realm, in all her splendour, looked composed from her tall throne at the end of the table.

Bella and Eli listened intently outside the door, trying to focus on the hushed voices within. The guests around the table spoke in quick and quiet voices making the atmosphere feel heavy and strained.

'Have you concluded your investigations, Loretta?' Aelfric spoke with a deep and strong accent.

'Indeed, I am most keen for answers. I have been extremely patient, but I must know why our beloved toadstool is running out of magic. This is for the good of the realm and for humankind, as you well know,' the queen added shrewdly.

Loretta Featherstone looked unusually flustered as she replied, 'Your Majesty, I am grateful for your patience while we conducted our investigations. Unfortunately, the situation is even more grave than I first feared. The humans we serve are becoming restless, with fewer and fewer of them believing in us and our magic. As you know, when a human no longer believes in us, we begin to fade in strength and eventually die. It is now taking too much magic to keep them believing in us, which is slowly killing our toadstool. It is my great worry that this will eventually spell the end for us too.'

Eli and Bella glanced nervously at each other behind the doorway. Their mouths hung open wide with shock and disbelief.

The queen reflected for a moment while the Council awaited her view. 'This is a grave situation indeed. I do not think our Council has faced a threat like this since the Great Goblin War,' she continued. 'We must fix this. What hope have you found?'

Professor Avery Curtis spoke next, with calm conviction. 'We do believe there is a cure, Your Majesty. The Celestial Wand.'

Morgan gasped. 'But that is merely legend, Avery?'

'Legends have their roots in truth, dear Morgan,' replied Aelfric, sagely. 'We need its power now more than ever, so perhaps now is the time to try.'

'Indeed,' encouraged Professor Curtis. 'It will take a near miracle to obtain, but if we manage it, we will be able to restore the realm's magic and more.'

The table was silent for a moment awaiting the queen's verdict.

'Very well,' the queen replied, with slight uncertainty. 'Do what you can to obtain the wand, but in the meantime, I will increase production at the ancient magic mine to ensure we have enough fairy dust in reserve.'

As the queen spoke, Eli stumbled forward clumsily, causing a just-audible scuff along the floor outside. Eden Briar turned towards the noise. Sharp as ever, Bella quickly pulled Eli back out of view before one of the Council members got up to investigate.

'We have to get out of here,' worried Bella. 'We'll get locked up if we're caught.' She grabbed Eli's hand and rushed them back towards the silver door. They peaked out discreetly to make sure the coast was clear, thankfully seeing that Mrs Nightingale was nowhere to be found. Seizing the opportunity, they dashed across the room to the fireplace portal. This time without hesitation, Bella and Eli dived head first through the illusion in front of them, landing with a thud back on the rug in the main library.

'That was close,' exhaled Eli.

Bella agreed. 'Too close. We better get back to the dorm room. The others will be worried and we need to tell them what's going on.' The pair darted towards the exit and scurried back though the network of underground tunnels, heading for the warmth of Kingfisher Hall without a moment to waste.

Chapter Seven

Bella and Eli crashed back through the door to Kingfisher Hall, cold, tired and breathless after running erratically through the network of unforgiving underground tunnels. All colour had drained from their faces, making them look pale as ghosts. Stunned by what they had witnessed, they couldn't wait to tell Felix and Marta what they had heard, although they didn't even know where to begin. The experience had left them shaken, speechless and suddenly unsure of their future, let alone that of the realm. Marta and Felix looked up, startled and worried at the state of them. They could tell that something was very wrong.

'Blimey, are you two okay?' exclaimed Felix.

Bella and Eli shook their heads. It was the only gesture they could manage given the shock of what they had just learnt. Marta rushed over, covering them both in warm blankets and giving them each a tight squeeze. She carefully guided them over to the middle of the room, sitting them down on the rug like they were made of fragile china and propping them up with large cushions. The friends formed a tight circle. When

Bella and Eli had caught their breath and calmed down enough to speak, Felix and Marta listened intently to everything they had just witnessed.

'That sounds awful. We're so glad you're both back safely,' said Marta, relieved. 'But rest assured, if the Fairy Council are aware of it, they will fix it. I think the best thing we can do now is to all get some sleep before our lessons start tomorrow.' Although she agreed it was a worrying thought that the realm could be running out of magic, she did wonder if Bella and Eli were slightly overreacting. She knew her brother, in particular, had a tendency to exaggerate and suspected this was the case again from his reaction. Marta, unlike her brother, had always been more relaxed and less up tight. Broadly speaking, she trusted things to work out as they were meant to and didn't think much warranted stressing over if it was outside of her own direct control. She also had complete and unwavering faith in the queen and Fairy Council, and knew that if the situation really was as bad as Bella and Eli feared, then they would have a plan to resolve things. That was their duty, after all. She encouraged the friends not to worry about it anymore and go to sleep. They had had a long day and were no doubt shattered. The best thing they could do now was to get a decent night's sleep before their very first lessons of the year. Although Bella and Eli felt less certain, they understood Marta's point and trusted her dearly. They reluctantly agreed to get some rest and each climbed into bed. After switching off their crystal lamps, the friends eventually fell asleep to the sound of Felix's gentle snoring.

After a few short hours of unsatisfying sleep, Bella tossed and turned under her duvet, battling the thoughts and worries that raced round her mind, making her restless. When she could no longer stand lying still, she got up quietly, careful not to wake the others, and wandered over to admire the moonlight and stars shining in through their bedroom window. As she stood there pondering everything they had overheard, her thoughts turned back to the book they had originally gone to find in the library. She wondered what secrets it held. Surely, it must contain something serious to be locked away in the enchanted section? It was a good distraction and felt much better to think about something controllable like this, instead of worrying about the fate of the realm.

Bella turned towards Eli who was still sleeping soundly. She noticed the mysterious book perched on his bedside table. Its heavy navy blue cover carried an unusual gold marking down its spine. As Bella admired it, the golden swan-like symbol seemed to shimmer back, as if personally calling out to her.

Eventually, curiosity got the better of her. Bella impulsively grabbed the book from the table and took it back to bed, sitting down with a huff. She held the peculiar book in her hands, feeling the soft grain of the leather cover and began flicking through the brown and crinkly age-worn pages. She wasn't sure what she would find inside, but that was perhaps part of the appeal at sneaking a look. She scanned the contents briefly, skipping over the larger chunks of text in the introduction, in favour of pictures and diagrams that explained the wonders of dream casting.

Like all fairies, Bella had always known that dream casting was a precarious and dangerous skill. It was a magical talent that took great patience and training to safely master, and something that very few fairies were naturally gifted at. It was the name given to the art of dream manipulation, a key magical tool that fairy godmothers used to help their human connections and hear their thoughts. Although the basics were taught at the academy, it wasn't until after graduation that the true strength of a dream cast was put to the test. This was when a fairy godmother finally bonded with their human connection. It was considered a great honour and the climax of every fairy godmother's graduation. During the ceremony, each graduate would scale the main tower of the academy and finally engrave their name into the crystal turret. When they landed back on the ground, they would discover the name of their human connection, or a symbol that represented them, tattooed on their body, in the same colour as their magical robes. This bond was sacred and connected the pair for life. It enabled the fairy godmother to sense and feel their human's thoughts and emotions through the strength of their magical bond. They would be able to visit their human within their dreams and travel through to the human realm to watch over them.

Although none of this was new to Bella, it was interesting to see it described in great detail through a series of sketches across the first few pages of the enchanted book. It was only as she progressed further through the chapters that she finally stumbled across the list of steps needed to complete the act itself. Bella read the ritual carefully, with burning curiosity.

The book explained that in order to start a dream cast, she would first need possession of a human object to provide a stable connection to the human realm. Luckily, Bella knew that Eli kept a closely guarded collection of small human objects, tucked away under balls of socks in his bedside drawer. She snuck over and borrowed a small red button that would have once sat proudly on a pretty school cardigan. She doubted the ritual would actually work without having graduated yet or being granted a human to protect; so she expected to be able to put the button back soon enough with Eli none the wiser to its disappearance.

Turning the page of the enchanted book, Bella read the instructions she must follow. The book explained the next step was to recite a special phrase to channel her fairy powers and begin the dream cast. Unsure if it was really wise, she was determined to try anyway. She took a deep breath and repeated the prescribed words in a whisper, just loud enough that only she could hear. 'I, Bella Brightheart, submit to the bond that rules all. Take me to the dream world to hear their call.'

Barely able to finish the chant, Bella felt herself slipping into unconsciousness, pulled down by a great invisible weight into something that felt like a deep meditative state. It felt like plummeting through a colourful, jumbled wormhole, sliding through the very fabric of time and space. The bizarre space smelt like vanilla and fresh cotton, comforting and hopeful. But at the same time it was loud and scary. All around, Bella could hear a buzz of scrambled thoughts competing for attention. They seemed to be a blur of wishes and pleas from all directions, making her head pound with pain. She tried to focus on one thought at a time until it gradually became clearer and louder than all the others, rising to the top of her awareness. Listening to the small and unsure voice echoing around her, Bella suddenly felt a great sadness in the pit of her stomach. She could sense that the voice belonged to a young and lonely girl, trying to sleep. Bella could feel her longing for something or someone, but parts of her thoughts were too blurry and difficult to make sense of. The girl seemed lost and was wishing to find somewhere she belonged.

Almost instantly, Bella felt herself being dragged upwards from the dream world she had landed in. Although she tried desperately to maintain the telepathic connection she had found, she couldn't stop herself from slipping away, helplessly floating upwards like an untethered balloon. As she started to regain consciousness, she felt a gentle squeeze on her shoulders. The strange bond had been shattered.

'Wake up, sleepy head,' Marta's voice rang from above. Bella opened her eyes to see her friends standing directly overhead, gently shaking her shoulders.

'You gave us a bit of a fright there, Bella. We thought you'd slipped into a sleeping curse or something,' chipped in a concerned Felix.

'I'm not quite sure what happened,' Bella yawned. 'One minute I was reading the magic book from the library, and the next I must have passed out.' She paused, trying to remember all the details she could. 'You guys aren't going to believe the most bizarre dream I've just had.'

Eli, who until now had been pacing the room, strolled over anxiously, gesturing to the clock on the wall. 'You'll have to tell us about it on the way. We don't want to be late for class.'

Chapter Eight

Excited by the prospect of finally starting lessons, the gang hurried through the network of underground tunnels leading from their dormitory back towards the main academy building. It was well known that the old tunnels seemed to have a mind of their own, making a habit of changing direction, seemingly at whim. Fortunately, the tunnels were behaving themselves this morning, guiding the young fairies in exactly the right direction towards their first lesson with minimal interference. Delighted by this spell of good fortune, Eli practically skipped along, humming the academy's anthem to himself until they finally arrived at their desired doorway, adorned with the gold plaque of 'Professor Melody Fairweather'.

As the friends entered, they noticed several of their classmates had already arrived. Eli was particularly disappointed to see the front desks had already been taken. Scarlett and Stella were perched there like peacocks, twirling their hair around their fingers while laughing at something Gale had just said. Everyone knew Gale wasn't especially funny, but it was impossible to deny that he sure had a funny way with the girls in his class. They all seemed besotted. Staring on disgruntled, Jupiter rolled his eyes, making the twins next to him giggle in unison.

The classroom was fairly small, but bustling with plants covered with ladybirds and exotic objects wherever they looked. Bright African patterns plastered the walls and the floors were littered with sculptures of animals in all shapes and sizes, creating a safari for the senses. Bella noticed there were three empty seats at the back of the room and quickly steered Eli and Felix over to claim them before anyone else arrived. As they got settled, they were greeted by a breathless Finn, who rushed in to grab the last empty seat just in front of them.

'Thank goodness, I thought I was going to be late,' panted a puffy and sweaty Finn, who had clearly overexerted himself to get there.

The class looked round at the antique cuckoo clock behind them, surprised that Professor Fairweather hadn't arrived yet, despite their lesson officially starting a few minutes ago.

'Maybe the Professor is running late,' shrugged Felix.

Suddenly, a high-pitched shriek echoed from Scarlett at the front of the classroom and she jumped onto her desk. 'Eeeeeeek! There's a great big hideous frog on the floor,' she screamed.

In an attempt to be chivalrous, Gale bent down to scoop up the frog, while Stella fanned Scarlett to calm her down. But despite his athletic appearance, Gale was too slow. The bright turquoise frog leapt competently through his hands to avoid capture and hopped furiously to the front of the classroom.

From within a whirlwind of fairy dust that exploded upwards from the floor like a tornado, the frog transformed before their eyes, revealing the familiar turquoise cloak of Professor Fairweather. 'Firstly,' Melody Fairweather started, 'I'm never late.' She winked at Felix and looked round the room at the stunned first years in front of her. Melody had always had a great sense of humour and often enjoyed a light-hearted prank, particularly on the unsuspecting younger students who idolised her. She continued, 'You'll soon learn how to shape shift like that too. Although, I appreciate some of you probably won't choose to become a frog.' She poked her tongue out at Stella teasingly.

'The skill of shape shifting is fundamental to our work helping humans. We can choose to appear to them in any form we can imagine, be it animal or human, which makes it a very powerful tool. We can also use it to help us realm jump, travelling through magical portals with ease to access the human world.' The class were silent, hanging onto her every word.

'For now though, we're going to start with the basics of realm jumping, teleportation. Who can tell me the magic ingredient for any kind of realm jumping, shape shifting or teleportation?' she asked her class.

Eli's hand shot up almost instantly from the back of the room. Professor Fairweather paused a moment to see if anyone else would volunteer. She didn't typically like overly keen students, but eventually conceded and nodded for Eli to answer.

'Fairy dust, Professor,' he responded eagerly.

Melody smiled. 'That's exactly right, Eli.' She tapped the little gold pouch full of fairy dust that was tied around her waist and continued, 'And to practise using fairy dust and getting to grips with the skill of realm jumping, we're going to start with the basics of shrinking in size and teleporting into a jar. So get up from your desks, grab yourselves a partner and come over to me for some fairy dust.'

In a flurry of excitement, the class rushed up from behind their desks to grab partners. Scarlett practically leapt on Gale; while Stella, somewhat disappointed, settled for pairing up with an equally reluctant Jupiter. As expected, the Summersong twins remained together; leaving Eli and Felix, and Bella and Finn, to pair up at the back of the classroom. In turn, Melody Fairweather walked round her class, giving each pair a glass jar and a sprinkling of fairy dust into each of their palms.

'Great, now you've got your partners and fairy dust, let's begin. Find a space around the room with your partner and place the glass jar down on the floor between you both,' instructed Professor Fairweather, giving them a moment to comply. 'The trick to any form of shape shifting and teleportation is to very clearly imagine exactly what you want to become and where you want to go. So close your eyes, take a deep breath and very clearly picture yourself in your mind's eye.' She paused to give her students time to process her instructions.

'Imagine yourself shrinking, right down to the ground, to the size of a teaspoon. Picture what the room looks like from down there. What can you see around you? How big will your desk look?' Melody paused once more. 'Now, take another deep breath and picture your tiny self in the glass jar in front of you. How might that feel? What would the world look like to you through the glass?' She took a moment to admire the students in front of her, eyes closed, taking in all of her instructions. 'Excellent. Now taking it in turns with your partner, you're going to complete the shape shift and teleportation. Keep that vision clear in your mind as you grip tighter onto the fairy dust,' she encouraged. 'When you're ready, take half of the fairy dust in your hand and blow it into the air in front of you as you picture where you want to go and what you want to become. As you hold tightly onto that thought, step through the sparkling cloud in front of you.'

A confident Jupiter took the plunge first out of the group. Although some of his classmates thought he was often a bit smug, he believed he had earned the right to be slightly arrogant by his studious nature and excellent academic record. His cool demeanour reflected this, remaining intact as he competently shrank to the size of a thimble and re-appeared in the glass in front of Stella. Once content Professor Fairweather had seen him, he used the remaining fairy dust in his hand to shape shift back to his original size and leant back against his desk with a smirk.

The class were undeniably impressed. But equally competitive and not wanting to be outdone by Jupiter, Stella was next in line to complete the test. She shrank into the jar and re-materialised with ease, causing a stunned Jupiter to blink twice. He certainly hadn't expected that. Maybe he'd finally met his match.

Scarlett, although slower than Stella, also managed the transformation first time. She then stood back by her desk chanting words of encouragement to Gale, who couldn't seem to get the hang of it and was getting visibly more frustrated. Despite being used to thinking about himself, Gale couldn't seem to shrink in size. It might have had something to do with his naturally inflated ego. No matter how hard he tried, he could only manage the teleportation part of the task. It caused him to dart repeatedly across the room at whiplash speed, knocking over statues and stacks of paper in his way. Tempest and Talia Summersong looked on at the mess, laughing silently to themselves through their telepathic twin connection. Together, they jumped into and out of the small glass jar with grace and ease, earning a nod of praise from Professor Fairweather.

At the back of the room, Eli and Felix began to try too. Felix could sense that Eli was nervous and gave him a thumbs up in encouragement. Eli took a deep breath and followed the Professor's instructions, elated to find himself in miniature form inside the glass jar on the floor. He smiled proudly to himself before teleporting back to full size, where he was greeted with a warm high five from Felix. Scarlett and Stella tutted loudly at his excellent performance and looked back to Gale, who had by now at least worked out how to shrink his ears and nose. Ignoring their negativity, Felix executed the skill next with a true Thunderbolt flourish, clicking his fingers and diving head first into the jar with a forward roll. He re-appeared to a well-deserved clap from the classroom.

Spurred on by the success of their friends, Bella and Finn took their turns next. Bella took a deep breath and gripped tightly onto the fairy dust, savouring the feeling of fine glittering sand. Just as Professor Fairweather had told them, she stepped into the magical cloud of fairy dust in front of her, feeling relieved to find herself in the small jar, just as she had imagined. She leapt back out from the jar to full size with a grin, gesturing to Finn to have a go too.

Feeling inspired, Finn tried to focus on the instructions. Within a moment, he found himself in tiny form on the floor, surrounded by large classroom objects. The scale of everything around him felt so overwhelming, making him panic and unable to focus on completing the teleportation. Luckily for him, Bella noticed and nudged the jar closer to him with a tap of her foot. He gratefully climbed in and took a deep breath to refocus, hoping no one else had noticed. When Finn finally re-appeared back to normal size in the classroom, he whispered his thanks to Bella, who smiled back sympathetically.

As the lesson came to a natural end, Melody Fairweather looked round proudly at her class. 'Well done, everyone. I know that trying new skills for the first time is not always easy, so I'm really proud of your effort and resilience.' She smiled, particularly at Gale and Finn. 'As you practise more and more, you'll find these skills get easier, and within no time at all, you'll be hopping round like me. So I really encourage you to practise, practise, practise…' The Professor's flow was interrupted by an efficient tap on the door. 'Come in,' she called, ever so slightly irritated.

The door opened to reveal a round, familiar face, framed with thin spectacles. 'Bella Brightheart?' enquired a less than jolly-looking Belinda Nightingale. 'Principal Featherstone would like to see you in her office.' Apprehensively, Bella got to her feet and followed Mrs Nightingale obediently out of the classroom. Her friends watched on concerned, surrounded by less sympathetic and more accusing glares from the rest of the class.

Chapter Nine

Guided by the diligent Mrs Nightingale, it didn't take long for Bella to arrive back at Principal Featherstone's office. In reality, the silent walk seemed to take an eternity, giving Bella's mind the chance to race round all the possibilities that could have brought her there. She slumped down in the waiting room as instructed and tried to block out her worries about being in trouble or having been caught sneaking around the library the other night. She really thought she'd got away with it, but perhaps Mrs Nightingale had been more perceptive than she'd thought.

Thankfully after only a few minutes, Bella heard Principal Featherstone call her through. She got to her feet and followed the sound of the principal's stern voice into her large round office. Although Bella had never been inside this room before, she knew it would feel opulent and was surely not disappointed. The office was a cross between a sanctuary and a museum, boasting an eclectic mix of modern art and ancient magical artefacts that had each clearly been carefully curated over the years to Loretta Featherstone's exacting taste. Bella looked around and admired each item as she slowly walked to the tulip-patterned sofa in the middle of the office and took a seat. She flopped down on the comfy cushions, at once remembering where she was and correcting her posture.

On the far side of the room, next to a square multi-headed lampshade tree, Principal Featherstone sat formidably behind a large marble desk. After making a final few taps on her bronze typewriter, she glanced up at Bella to offer a half-smile and rose to join her on the sofa. Today, Principal Featherstone's hair perfectly matched her deep orange cloak and irises, but her pale silver skin seemed more strained and paper-thin than usual. As Bella watched her trademark stilettos click efficiently across the old wooden floorboards, she thought she seemed stressed but was trying her best to hide it.

'Thank you for seeing me, Bella,' began Principal Featherstone. 'May I offer you some tea?' She gestured to the delicate tea set sat on the mahogany table in front of her. Bella was hit instantly by the pleasant fragrance of jasmine and orange blossoms coming from the steaming china teapot. 'Yes, please,' Bella replied.

Loretta poured tea for them both, also dolloping a heaped teaspoon of honey into each cup for good measure. 'You may be wondering why I called you in here today?' she questioned, probing Bella to come clean. When Bella offered no reply she continued, 'I often have the pleasure of teaching students with great potential, like yourself, but I find that the trouble with such potential is that it can be channelled into both positive and negative pursuits.' Principal Featherstone sipped her tea, peering over the china cup to give Bella another chance to fill the silence.

Sensing that Bella would be a tough nut to crack, Loretta persevered. 'Now I understand from my trusted secretary, Mrs Nightingale, that you found yourself alone in the enchanted section of the library the other night. I believe you were supposedly searching for Marta Evenstar's pet hedgehog, Luna. Is that right?' She arched an eyebrow, prompting a short and saccharine reply from Bella, 'Yes, principal.'

'Hmmm. Now, while I don't doubt you would always tell me the truth,' Loretta replied sternly, 'I have to say, I am not entirely convinced that is the full story.' She stared inquisitively at Bella and continued, 'You see, call it intuition after so many decades running this academy, but I sense when young fairies might be getting themselves into trouble, and even if it is to help a friend, it is my job to keep you all safe. The enchanted section of the library, like many off-limit areas of our academy, can be a dangerous place to explore, especially alone, and especially without the proper training and experience to protect yourself. Do you understand?'

Bella nodded. 'Good,' smiled Principal Featherstone. 'The thing is, you seem to remind me so much of a younger version of myself that while I'm sure you were up to something mischievous, I also have no doubt you did so with the best of intentions,' she sighed. 'I am also certain that you have great potential, especially considering your performance in class this morning and willingness to help your friends. So my advice to you is this; stay on the right path and you will achieve great things here, but please don't make a habit of being called into my office. Do I make myself clear?'

'Yes, principal,' replied Bella respectfully, hoping to show she had taken Loretta's warning seriously. Loretta smiled back approvingly. 'Very well. It was a pleasure speaking to you, Bella. You better head on your way now to the Great Hall. It's lunchtime and your friends will be missing you.'

When Bella entered the Great Hall, she saw her friends had already grabbed a table and started eating. They all looked relieved to see her and waved over for her to join them. As soon as she sat down, Marta scooped her up into a hug. 'Eli and Felix told me you got called in to see Principal Featherstone. Are you okay?'

'Yeah, it wasn't too bad,' shrugged Bella, grateful for the sympathy of her friends. 'We just had a cup of blossom tea and she mainly told me to behave myself. I think we got away with it this time, but one thing is for sure, we'll have to be much more careful if we're sneaking around again in future.'

Felix and Eli nodded in agreement. 'I'm really sorry I got you into trouble, Bella,' apologised Eli. Bella smiled back at him. 'Don't worry about it, Eli. It's nothing I can't handle and it's always worth it to help a friend.'

The Great Hall was, as always, spectacular. It was very common for it to be decorated and themed for a special occasion, or to celebrate a particular culture of the human or magical realm. Principal Featherstone actively encouraged this to be done regularly to teach her students about the wider world and the importance of embracing other cultures. She was well known throughout the magical kingdom for being an advocate of cohesion and unity, challenging the magical community to be more accepting and celebrating of their differences, even spearheading the movement to allow fairy godmothers of elvish descent to study at the academy.

This afternoon, the hall was decorated fit for a harvest festival, celebrating all that autumn had to offer. Large canopies of burnt-orange leaves were draped across the high vaulted ceiling, suspended like bunting. Piles of autumn vegetables decorated the large round wooden tables scattered around the room for students to mingle and feast together. All around, hungry students gathered after a busy morning of lessons to enjoy an autumnal feast of warming honey and parsnip soup or marrow stew. Yet for the sweet-toothed fairies, pudding was just as important and no meal was ever complete without dessert. Magical, self-steering silver carts wheeled round the room serving heaps of spiced pumpkin pie with maple clotted cream and candied chestnuts.

As the gang tucked into a hearty meal, their conversation turned to lighter topics, briefing Marta on all the gossip from their first-ever class at the academy. Marta laughed knowingly. 'Did Professor Fairweather shape shift into a frog by any chance?'

'It was the coolest thing ever!' replied Felix, without missing a beat.

'And Scarlett totally freaked out and nearly stomped on her,' added Eli.

'Poor Gale has got his work cut out for him with that girl, for sure,' chuckled Bella, peering round to look at Scarlett's table. Predictably, Scarlett was sat next to Gale and Stella, trying to muster extra sympathy from the Summersong twins and Jupiter after her morning ordeal. Scarlett caught Bella's eye and threw a suspicious glance back in her direction, forcing Bella to look away quickly.

'That was delicious,' exclaimed Eli as he shovelled the last crumb of pie into his mouth. Felix agreed with a burp.

'Eww, gross you guys,' Marta looked over in disgust. As she turned back, she noticed the familiar yellow cloak of Neptune as he nervously approached their table from the north entrance of the hall.

'Hi everyone,' smiled Neptune, waving. 'I hope your lessons got off to a good start this morning.' He greeted the table warmly, paying particular attention to Marta, who blushed in response.

'All good, thanks, Neptune. How's your morning been?' she replied.

'Not too bad, thanks. I've been out tending to the unicorns today. They're quite playful and mischievous characters, so they keep stampeding through the piles of leaves I rake up. They seem to think it's a charming game, but I'm the one that has to clean them all up again.' Neptune spoke so passionately about his job that it was impossible not to admire him. His commitment and dedication were truly impressive. Marta, also an animal lover, swooned as he continued, 'Anyway, I'm not here to bore you about the grounds today. Marta, I was actually wondering if you were planning on going to the wish wielding competition tomorrow?'

Bella cut in, 'What exactly is a wish wielding competition? Sounds exciting!'

'Oh it is,' replied Neptune. 'It's basically a magical battle between some of the most skilful final-year students. Spectacular to see and very popular. I wouldn't be surprised if the whole realm turns up to watch.' He returned his gaze to Marta, hoping for an answer to his previous question. Her blush deepened, understanding that Neptune was trying, very sweetly, to ask her out on a date. She replied, 'I certainly am going. But I was actually planning on taking this lot to the competition.' She gestured to the gang round the table. 'It'll be the first time they've ever seen wish wielding in real life, you see.' Sensing that Neptune seemed slightly deflated at the idea of a group date, she added, 'It'd be lovely to see you there though Neptune, and I'd love to take you up on your offer of a tour of the grounds sometime.'

Neptune smiled back at her. 'I'd love that too, Marta. Anyway, I better get back to those pesky unicorns.' He laughed. 'See you all tomorrow.'

Marta waved him farewell and called back after him, 'See you later, Neptune.'

As soon as Bella was sure Neptune was out of earshot, she turned to Marta with a wide grin. 'He is so into you, Marta!'

Marta rolled her eyes.

'All I'm saying is that you two would make a lovely couple,' Bella teased.

'And that would get you off our backs too,' chimed in Eli, just as the class bell rung to signal the end of lunchtime.

'Luckily for me, it's time for us all to get to class,' giggled Marta. 'Good luck for your first dream casting lesson. Don't be late… Professor Curtis hates that.'

Bella gave Marta a conspiratorial look to let her know their discussion about boys would be continued later. In a rush not to be late, the friends quickly got to their feet and headed straight for Professor Curtis' classroom.

Chapter Ten

Bella, Eli and Felix arrived through the classroom door with moments to spare. As Marta had warned, Professor Avery Curtis was as punctual as ever. He was already stood at the front of the class, counting down the seconds on his antique pocket watch while tapping his foot against the wooden floorboards to mimic its rhythm. As soon as he reached zero, he flipped the watch shut and slipped it back into the pocket of his purple waistcoat. With a simple flick of his wrist, the classroom door slammed closed behind them.

'Good afternoon, everyone,' Professor Curtis spoke with calm authority, capturing the class's attention instantly. His classroom felt older and more traditional than Professor Fairweather's, but was embellished with a collection of common and rare musical instruments that would make even the most avid musician jealous. He stood by his chalkboard, scrawling across it in large messy letters. 'Dream Casting.' He underlined the text twice with thick white chalk, before turning back to address his class. 'Who can tell me what it is?'

Clearly wanting to impress their slightly intimidating new teacher, several hands shot up across the classroom, including Eli's. Professor Curtis scanned the room, instead choosing to pick someone who did not have their hand up. His gaze landed on Stella, volunteering her to respond.

She cleared her throat. 'It's about sharing dreams, isn't it, Professor?'

'That's mostly correct,' Professor Curtis nodded. 'But more than that, it is about dream manipulation. This makes it a key skill for all fairy godmothers to learn to help hear the thoughts of their human connections.' He continued, 'As you know, you won't get your actual human connection until after you graduate from the academy. So for now, we're going to create a safe space where you can all practise the basics of dream casting, by visiting each other's dreams.' The mood in the classroom fizzed with nervous excitement.

Initiating another knowledge test, Professor Curtis asked the class, 'Does anyone know the significance of a shared dream cast?' This time around, fewer hands were raised. Tempest and Talia Summersong held their arms up high and confidently, eager to respond. Along with their elder brother Neptune, they had grown up surrounded by the myths and legends of fairy folklore and tales from 'the old realm' before the Great Goblin

War. They responded together when prompted, 'Shared dreams are the most powerful kind.'

Professor Curtis smiled. 'Indeed, girls. A shared dream is the most powerful kind of dream, where fairy godmothers collectively dream together. It can be used to channel large amounts of magic, but that can also be very dangerous and extremely draining, so it is traditionally only used in times of great crisis, such as the Great Goblin War of the old realm, or where multiple human connections are in danger and need our help.' A sombre atmosphere fell over the class as they understood the weight of their chosen path and the importance of their training. The Professor continued, 'So today, we are going to try a very basic shared dream, so you can begin to understand how to interact with the dream world.' Trying to make the atmosphere feel more upbeat again, he added, 'Did everyone bring a small object they own with them, as requested?'

The class nodded. Bella looked quizzically at the Professor and asked, 'Why is the object so important? And why does it have to be something we own?'

Professor Curtis was momentarily stunned, mostly impressed, and slightly puzzled by Bella's thoughtful question. The object chosen was of fundamental importance to any dream cast, but was simply not something that first years typically thought to ask.

After a moment he responded, 'To dream cast in the most effective way, you need to use an object owned by the person or fairy whose dreams you wish to visit. Ideally this object would be something sentimental, as this will provide a stronger connection to the dream world, but for the purposes of today, any object you have will do. As you will experience, the dream world can be a bit messy and confusing, so using a random object can make the process more difficult. To prevent the dream cast being too disorientating, the personal object will act like a tether to help pull you back to your own thoughts and consciousness.'

Bella nodded thoughtfully and began to unwrap the burgundy bracelet woven around her wrist for the dream cast. She thought back to the confusion of her own experience of dream casting the night before in their dormitory. Professor Curtis' explanation made a lot of sense. She only wished their magical book had gone into as much detail. It might have saved her one almighty headache.

The class pushed their tables and chairs to the edge of the room, making way in the centre for them all to gather. One by one, they each placed their personal objects on the floor in the middle, led by Professor Curtis, who placed down a brightly coloured chequered bow tie. Bella followed with her bracelet, along with

Felix's sweatband, a paperclip from Eli's collection and a thimble from Finn. Tempest and Talia each laid down a velvet hair tie that matched the colours of their olive-green and lilac cloaks. Stella added a spiky silver star-shaped hair clip to the collection, followed by Scarlett who made a great fuss of taking off her gold signet ring and placing it delicately onto the floor on top of a silk napkin. Slightly reluctantly, Jupiter placed down his diary, hoping that using such a personal object would help him to excel in the exercise ahead. Finally, Gale stepped into the centre. He had clearly forgotten to bring any personal object of note, so decided to improvise by throwing in one of his tattered trainers.

Somewhat unimpressed, Professor Curtis rolled his eyes at Gale but choose to stay silent. Ever since his own school years, he had always been deemed a bit of an outcast. His passion for classical music and pedantic tendencies, combined with his natural flamboyance, had always made him a target for bullies. He still carried this trauma around today which manifested as a dislike for jocks and general scepticism about their performance in his classes. Shrugging off his annoyance, he instructed the class to lie down in a circle with their heads towards the middle of the room where their personal objects were. 'The circle will form a protective charm while we are in the dream world and away from our physical bodies,' he explained. 'I am also going to play some music, which will act as a strong tether to the present moment. If at any time you feel overwhelmed by the experience, focus on the music and your breathing and you will begin to float back to consciousness.' Professor Curtis switched on a surprisingly modern-looking record player, sending his favourite piece of classical music echoing around the room. Feeling peaceful again, he joined the circle with the students and instructed, 'Everyone take a deep breath and repeat after me, inserting your own name as appropriate. I, Avery Curtis, submit to the bond that rules all. Take me to the dream world to hear their call.'

As the class repeated the magical chant, they each felt a great heaviness within that pulled them down into unconsciousness. Bella had already known the chant and exactly what to expect. This time around, she felt more prepared for the disorientating world that would greet her. She could still smell the familiar scents of cotton and vanilla, but the noises that surrounded her were more distant and less oppressive than before. She also seemed to slip more quickly through the wormhole she was in and felt shocked to suddenly find herself awake again, back in the same position on the classroom floor as only a moment before. Professor Curtis had already arrived too and was standing by his record player. As she looked round the classroom, he caught her eye with an uneasy expression that Bella didn't quite understand.

Although on first glance, everything in the classroom seemed to be more or less the same as before, something had changed. Bella's vision was surrounded by a milky-white, slightly shiny film that made the world look fuzzy and blurred around the edges, almost as if looking through a frosty glass window. Although the difference was subtle, it also made everything feel more fragile and temporary. After several more moments, her classmates began to wake around her, rubbing their eyes or holding their sore heads after their own confusing journey.

'Welcome to the dream world everyone,' said Professor Curtis. 'Take a few moments to get used to your surroundings. I know it can be quite a lot the first time around and you may even feel slightly nauseous.' After giving them some time to breath, he continued, 'Once you feel like you've got your bearings, try to stand up and experiment with how you can interact with the dream world and objects around you. Remember, your own imagination is your only limit,' he added encouragingly.

Bella, who had already acclimatised to her new surroundings, was first to stand up. She imagined a dainty burgundy butterfly and held the vision sharply in her mind until she could practically see every detail of what it looked like and how it moved. When she opened her eyes, she was ecstatic to see the real thing, fluttering in front of her. Eli gasped next to her.

'You're a natural there, aren't you Bella?' praised a somewhat uncertain Professor Curtis. 'It's almost like you've done this before.' He arched a sceptical brow.

'Thanks, Professor. This is amazing!' beamed Bella, unaware of the Professor's uneasy tone.

Taking Bella's lead, the rest of the class began to experiment with manipulating the space around them. Felix, coming from a realm-renowned family of highly skilled dream casters, was also unsurprisingly a natural. Within minutes, he had created a cascade of giant bubbles that floated up towards the ceiling, even managing to scoop up Eli inside one of the magical spheres. As Eli floated towards the classroom ceiling within the giant iridescent bubble, he imagined a sharp silver pin and brought it to life in his hand. He popped the giant bubble prison that had trapped him and landed back on the floor with a thump, causing everyone, Eli included, to burst out in fits of laughter.

Even Finn, who hadn't got off to a good start with classes so far, was managing to create magic in the dream cast. He was currently tending to a small bonsai tree he had created. Stella and Scarlett were stood next to him, using the power of thought to change each other's hair colour through every shade of the rainbow, trying to guess which colour Gale would like best, and which clashed least with their magical robes.

Oblivious to this, Gale sat on the floor, legs outstretched in front of him, trying to summon a replica of his tattered trainer back onto his bare foot. Jupiter sat nearby and watched, but thought it would be much more fun to use the dream cast to prank his best friend. Each time Gale managed to create a new shoe for himself, Jupiter used his imagination to change the shoe in Gale's hand, right before he could put it on. This time, holding a large pink stiletto, Gale looked baffled.

Ignoring the boys misbehaving across the room, a shimmer caught the corner of Bella's eye. She walked over to the marble mantlepiece by the window where it had come from, and noticed a small rose-gold pocket watch. Bella picked it up. It felt warm to touch and strangely familiar. Without thinking, she slipped it into her robe pocket.

Professor Curtis looked round the room, finally comfortable his students had now had a good chance to dream cast. He felt it was the right time to wrap things up and end their first class on a high note, so instructed his students, 'We're now going to leave the dream world and head back to the real classroom. Lie back down where you originally were, take a deep breath and focus on the music in the background of your mind. You will feel the pull of your own object pulling you back…'

That was the last Bella heard before waking up again back in her own body on the floor of the classroom. Her classmates stirred around her, also regaining consciousness. She looked over at her friends, Eli and Felix, who smiled back at her. Spirits were high all across the class after an excellent lesson, until unfortunately, poor Finn interrupted the moment by vomiting across the floor.

'There's always one, isn't there?' half chuckled Professor Curtis. 'I think that's enough excitement for today. Be sure to read chapters one to five of your text book before next week.' As Professor Curtis helped Finn, the class was dismissed. Bella, Eli and Felix headed back to Kingfisher Hall, after a long and exciting first day of lessons.

Chapter Eleven

Exhausted after a long day of lessons, the gang were relieved to be back in the warmth and comfort of their dormitory at Kingfisher Hall. They sat on their neighbouring beds to discuss the day's events, wrapped up in layers of snuggly blankets and each cradling cups of caramel hot chocolate with mini marshmallows.

'So, how did your first-ever dream cast go, Eli?' asked Marta eagerly, blowing her mug to cool down the velvety hot chocolate.

'It was good once we'd finished it, but the whole experience gave me such a headache,' he replied.

Felix agreed. 'No wonder poor Finn vomited everywhere.'

Marta smiled sympathetically. 'Yeah, it can take a while to get used to, but it does get much easier each time, I promise.'

'Is that what you felt like when you went through to the dream world the other night, Bella?' asked Eli. 'I'm not surprised you looked so poorly after.' He gave her a gentle smile. 'Sorry I was so unsympathetic.'

Bella nodded. 'That's okay, Eli. Yeah, it was the same for me the first time round. Everything was so confusing. It felt like being trapped in the dark on a noisy merry-go-round. Thankfully, today was much better. Although, I'm not sure if it was because I was using my own object this time, or just getting more used to it.'

The friends paused thoughtfully. Felix broke the silence first, noisily draining his mug of cocoa and slurping down the final marshmallow.

'I think it might be time we got some rest, don't you all agree?' suggested Marta. 'We've got another big day tomorrow. I can't wait for you all to see some wish wielding! You're going to love it!'

'Sounds good, sis,' agreed Eli, gathering up everyone's mugs and placing them back on a serving tray by the door. Thankfully, another perk of studying at the academy was not having to do any washing up. As well as a fully catered offering, the academy also had bountiful staff on hand to make sure the students could focus solely on their studies. Eli left the mugs by the door ready to be collected later, along with a small, handwritten thank-you note for their maid. Felix let out a big sleepy yawn, while Bella turned out their crystal lamp, ready to go to sleep after a long and tiring day. Before long, the room was lit only by a thin sliver of moonlight streaming in through their window, and the only sound was, predictably, Felix's easy snoring.

At some point in the middle of the night, Bella awoke, restless again and unable to go back to sleep. Her mind raced with thoughts of her lessons that day, excited with how she had performed and eager to learn more. Given how much easier her last dream cast had been, she wondered what it would be like if she were to try it again. Could she enter other dreams? Perhaps even those of her friends sleeping beside her?

Feeling even more impulsive than usual, Bella made up her mind to try the dream cast again. For as long as she could remember, she had always been a stubborn and determined fairy. Ever since she was little, she had been relentless when she had her mind set on something. It was a trait her parents had often found particularly challenging while she was growing up, but it also gave them great confidence that she would achieve wonderful things at the academy. Bella thought of her parents and smiled fondly. Making them proud meant the world to her and they were so happy to see her following her dream of becoming a fairy godmother.

After a moment's daydream, Bella resumed her plan. She grabbed the large dream casting book from their hiding place in Eli's wardrobe and brought it back over to her bedside. Although impulsive, Bella was also smart. She was keen to put everything she had learnt earlier from Professor Curtis into practice, and now knew that it was important to take precautions to protect her physical body while in the dream world. Thinking on her feet, she found a packet of stale biscuits that Felix had been storing for a late-night snack and crumbled these into a fine sand, scattering this around her bed to form a protective circle.

The next thing she knew she needed was a sentimental object to make the link between the dream world and magical realm easier to navigate. Looking around for something suitable, she felt a strange warmth in her side and remembered the small rose-gold pocket watch she had retrieved from her earlier adventure. Bella wasn't sure if it would work, but as it had already travelled from the dream world, she thought it would be worth a try.

Confident she had everything she needed, Bella lay back in bed and closed her eyes, ready to try the dream cast once more. She took a deep breath and whispered the magic words into the darkness of the room around her: 'I, Bella Brightheart, submit to the bond that rules all. Take me to the dream world to hear their call.'

At once, Bella felt herself falling through the mattress and sliding down a twisting path of unconsciousness into an endless abyss below. Again, a symphony of chattering voices echoed and boomed around her, bouncing off imaginary walls and wrestling for her attention. Bella gripped the pocket watch tighter, hoping it would guide her safely to the dream world she sought. It seemed to be working, and after what felt like minutes, the distant noises fell silent. They were gradually replaced with trills of melodic birdsong, and the fresh scent of spring. When everything finally felt still and calm again, she took a moment to feel the world around her, realising that she had landed gently on her back with something soft and moist underneath.

Bella opened her eyes to see where she was. She had landed on a plush carpet of grass, blanketed with a delicate layer of dewdrops. She sat up and admired the field around her, the dew sparkling like a sheet of diamonds across the lush countryside. She ran her hand through the rich emerald grass and picked up a buttercup, admiring its brilliant yellow shine. In the distance, the first streaks of warm orange sun were peaking over the horizon, teasing the start of a beautiful day.

Glancing around the meadow, Bella noticed a quiet woodland clearing, framed by rows of old and wise oak trees. It reminded her of the hollow where their fairy portal stood, used for realm jumping to and from the human world. She pondered if it was in fact the very same hollow. Perhaps she had indeed fallen into one of her friend's dreams and would shortly see Marta prancing through the spring meadow, without a care in the world.

Spurred on from her earlier success, Bella decided to explore the dream world she had found herself in. She skipped along the field, using her new-found dream casting talents to magically create bursts of colourful wildflowers wherever she stepped. Whoever's dream she had ended up in, she at least hoped to spread them some joy while they slept. It was after all, the very least a fairy godmother could do.

The sun continued to rise high above the horizon, turning from burnt orange, to bright gold, and casting warm light in all directions across the rolling hills of surrounding countryside. Further in the distance, Bella noticed what seemed to be a strange group of large grey rocks, stacked high in an odd formation to form a large and unusual circle. It was something Bella had never actually seen before, but had read about while growing up. She knew it only by its name in the human realm – Stonehenge.

Understanding the significance of this landmark, Bella was now certain that their magical portal was nearby, which meant she had likely landed in the dream of someone who knew of the existence of fairies. Tenacious as ever, she decided to investigate and continued down to the small forest opening in front of her. As she approached the hollow, large trees loomed over her. Their branches stretched out like arms, ready to warn off unwanted guests. Fortunately for Bella, they seemed to recognise her, shaking their leaves gently in greeting and opening the mouth of the hollow wider for her to safely pass through.

Stepping inside the hollow was like stepping into another world. The space was much larger than Bella had expected. Untouched by the warm light of the sun, the atmosphere felt cold and damp. It was also quiet, with even the harmonious trills of birdsong unable to penetrate the dense greenery. Although dark, Bella could make out the middle of the hollow, where two large oak trees proudly stood. They seemed to frame a perfect rectangle of thin air that seemed too suspicious to be accidental. Bella was convinced it must be a dream world replica of their magical fairy realm portal. She wandered over to take a closer look, searching for remnants of used fairy dust or any fairy markings carved into the trees that stood guard.

As Bella explored, she heard a sudden and sharp crack behind her. The sound of a snapping branch echoed around the silent hollow, making her spin round in shock. To her surprise, a young girl stood in front of her, equally unsure, and waving a long pointy stick in her direction.

'Who are you?' demanded the girl. Bella stared back quizzically, forcing her to continue, 'What are you doing here?'

After a moment of stunned silence, Bella responded openly to the human stood in front of her. 'I'm Bella. What's your name?'

'I'm Darcy,' she replied shyly. The dark-haired girl seemed to sense that Bella wasn't a threat and slowly lowered her pointy stick.

'Nice to meet you, Darcy,' Bella smiled warmly. 'It's a lovely dream you have here.' She noticed the unusual turquoise gemstone hung around Darcy's neck. 'And that's a beautiful necklace you have. It looks almost magical.'

'Thanks,' Darcy replied somewhat less cautiously. With a slight shine to her hazel eyes, she added proudly, 'It was a gift from my mother. She said it would protect me and keep away bad dreams, so I always keep it close.'

Bella smiled. For some unknown reason, she suddenly felt a tightness tugging at her chest. It reminded her of sadness, and how she thought Darcy might be feeling now talking about her mother. Bella replied tenderly, 'This is going to sound a bit strange, but I think I am meant to protect you too. I think that might be why I've been brought here.'

Although she didn't understand why, something about this statement also felt true to Darcy. For some strange and unknown reason, Bella felt warm, safe, and like someone she could trust.

'Are you a fairy?' she asked Bella spontaneously.

Bella was thrown by Darcy's thoughtful question, but replied honestly. 'Yes. I'm a fairy godmother. But how do you know about us?'

'My mother always told me you were real,' Darcy answered, as if it were obvious. 'She always told me that we each have a fairy godmother to look after us, but only if we believed in them.' She held back tears as she spoke. 'The only trouble is, since my mother passed away, I've been worried I would stop believing in magic all together.'

Filled with overwhelming sadness and a strong urge to protect Darcy, Bella pulled her into a tight embrace. Although it didn't make sense to either of them, the pair felt a strange connection. Like they were always meant to know each other. Like it was written in the stars.

As Bella pulled away, she started to feel faint, almost like she was floating. Much to Darcy's concern, Bella's colour started to drain too. She was slowly but surely fading, slipping away from the dream world and back to reality.

'You're turning see-through, Bella!' panicked Darcy.

Bella's speech faded next. 'I think I'm waking up Darcy…'

Not ready to lose her new friend, Darcy grabbed onto Bella's burgundy sleeve, throwing them both off balance. They toppled backwards together into the gap between the giant oak trees, tumbling through the hidden fairy portal.

Chapter Twelve

With a sudden jolt, Bella awoke from the dream world she had been in, jumping at the sound of a loud thud on the floor next to her bed. As she peered over the edge, she was shocked to see Darcy, asleep on the plush rug next to her. She remembered Darcy grabbing onto her within the dream world, but had no idea it was possible for a human to cross over into the fairy realm. The dream casting book certainly hadn't mentioned it. Despite this, she felt a strange sense of relief to see her lying there. She was now more certain than ever that it was her job to look after Darcy and she was determined to find a way to get her back home safely.

Bella climbed out of bed, carefully draping a blanket over Darcy to keep her warm. She knew how disorientating the transition from the dream world could be, so wanted to make sure she would be as comfortable as possible when she awoke. It would be shocking enough to wake up somewhere she wasn't expecting, let alone in the magical realm, so Bella hoped to make the realisation as gentle as possible. She knelt down next to Darcy and leant over, carefully shaking her shoulders to see if she was ready to wake up.

Disturbed by the loud thud she had just heard, Marta startled awake and looked round to check on her friends. Alarmed at the sight of Bella cradling a human on the floor, she was at Bella's side in an instant, calling to the boys to wake up too. They had no clue how it had happened, but they knew they definitely couldn't afford to get caught with a human in school. They would surely be expelled, or perhaps even worse. They quickly gathered, forming a close circle around Bella and their new guest.

'What in fairy realm's name has happened here, Bella?' exclaimed an increasingly worried Marta, her voice building in pitch to a screech.

'It's a long story,' Bella sighed. 'When I couldn't sleep last night, I tried to dream cast again using the pocket watch I found in class. It took me to a dream world on the human side of the fairy portal, where I met Darcy.' She gestured to the girl lying on the floor between them. 'I can't explain it, but I think she might be my human connection. I think I'm supposed to keep her safe.'

An angry Eli scoffed back sarcastically, 'Well, you've done a fantastic job of that so far, Bella.' It was unlike him to be so unkind, but he was also bad at handling high-pressure situations. With his heritage as a half-elf, it already felt like he had had to work harder than anyone else to prove himself and to be accepted in the academy. He would never dream of coming so close to expulsion.

Bella's shoulders slumped in defeat. She also felt like she had failed as a fairy godmother, before she'd even started. She wished more than anything she could fix things. Marta sensed Bella's pain and squeezed her shoulders in support. 'All that matters is that you're both safe,' comforted Marta. Bella was grateful for her friend. She was always the one to bring love and positivity when it was needed most. 'Now, we just have to work out how to get her home,' Marta added, like it would be a walk in the park.

'You're right, Marta,' agreed Felix. 'We can do this. Together.'

Eli let out a long sigh and looked over at Bella apologetically. 'I'm sorry, Bella. I didn't mean what I said. Felix is right, we'll fix this together.'

As the friends started to discuss the few options they could think of, Darcy stirred beside them. She slowly opened her hazel eyes, blinking a few times to adjust to the light. As her vision became clearer, she was shocked to see Bella and three other strangers staring down at her with concern. They also seemed to shimmer slightly, just like Bella, so she guessed they must also be fairies. Her mother had always warned her not to eat cheese before bed or she would get nightmares. She wished she had listened. What a bizarre dream she'd found herself in.

'Hi Darcy,' Bella greeted her warmly, treating her gently like fine china.

'Wh-where am I?' Darcy asked timidly, rubbing the back of her head.

'This might come as a bit of a shock,' Bella continued slowly to make sure Darcy was fully conscious and following along. 'You travelled back with me last night through a magical portal in your dream.' She paused, taking her time to make sure Darcy understood. 'You're now in the fairy realm.'

Darcy was left pale and speechless. She needed a moment to process what Bella had said. Surely this couldn't be real? Yet an uncomfortable feeling in the pit of her stomach told her it was.

In stark contrast to Bella's gentle approach, Felix was overly eager to welcome Darcy. He had only ever heard tales of humans from his famous family, but never actually met one before and was keen to make an excellent first impression. It felt like he was meeting royalty. He bounded his way to the front of the group like an excited puppy. 'Welcome to the Hummingbird

Academy for Fairy Godmothers,' he declared proudly, with an uncharacteristically uncool bow, 'I'm Felix.'

Ignoring Felix's goofiness, Marta smiled warmly. 'And I'm Marta.' She nudged Felix back out of the way to give Darcy some breathing space. 'Take your time sitting up, sweetie.'

Dazed and still slightly disorientated, Darcy slowly sat up, taking in the magnificence of the room around her. She had never seen such a vivid tapestry of colours, and impossibly, everything looked even brighter and more colourful than the dream world she had just come from.

'Umm, hi,' replied Darcy timidly, somewhat unsure of her new company and surroundings. 'So this is really real? I'm really here?'

Bella nodded softly. Eli offered Darcy an outstretched hand. 'Hi Darcy, I'm Eli,' he gave her a nervous smile. Although he was anxious about how much trouble they might get in if they ever got caught, he didn't want Darcy to worry. He had always been raised to be welcoming of others and show excellent hospitality, so more than anything, he wanted her to feel comfortable while she was there. 'Don't worry about anything, Darcy. We're going to help you get home,' he said, trying his best to comfort her.

For the second time in a short while, Darcy didn't understand why, but knew deep down in her heart that she could trust Bella and her fairy friends. As if reading her mind, Bella affirmed what she already knew. 'I promise we'll keep you safe, Darcy,' smiled Bella encouragingly. 'And I think I might have something that belongs to you?' She pulled out the small, rose gold pocket watch from her burgundy cloak pocket and offered it over to Darcy.

'That's my mother's watch!' Darcy exclaimed, amazed and confused. 'I thought I'd lost it. How did you find it?'

'I'm not quite sure, Darcy, but I think I was meant to find it,' explained Bella, 'I think it helped me find you too. That's how I ended up in your dream.'

Darcy paused thoughtfully, then nodded as if she already knew it to be true. 'Why don't you keep it safe for me then?' she asked Bella softly. 'Keep it close so you can always find me.'

'It would be my pleasure.' Bella felt a swell of pride as she tucked the watch safely back into her pocket. 'Now, we just need to figure out how to get you home. We might need to go back to the library for some research.' She looked round at her friends, seeking agreement or any other suggestions.

Marta interrupted. 'That's a great plan, Bella, but the academy will be bustling by now. We will have to wait until later after the wish wielding competition, or at least while everyone is distracted there.'

'Good idea! Then we can make our escape,' nodded Felix. 'What do you say, Darcy? Are you ready to see some real fairy magic? You might as well experience the realm while you're here?'

Darcy felt a small thrill at the thought of seeing real-life fairy magic up close, just as her mother had described. 'That sounds like quite an adventure. Count me in!'

'Brilliant,' Marta beamed. 'But you can't go out looking like that! It's far too human. You're going to need a disguise to blend in.' She chuckled. 'Luckily, we have some time to kill before we need to leave, so I have ample opportunity to work my magic. I hope you like pink!' Marta strolled over to her huge wardrobe, rummaging through seemingly endless racks of outfits until she found the perfect look. Settling for a pair of sleek pink trousers, with a matching top, Marta then pulled out another deep pink cloak and wrapped Darcy up in the soft, thick, velvety fabric. Darcy felt anxious but excited. She hoped the disguise would be good enough to conceal her true identity and that her mother's gemstone necklace would give her luck and keep her safe. Noticing Darcy's beautiful necklace, Marta draped it over the outside of her cloak as a finishing touch. 'Every fairy likes to show off a bit of personality.' Marta winked, approving of her skilled disguise. 'Much better.'

She then turned to her brother Eli, who was nervously pacing across the floor. 'Eli, remember, if we're going to pull this off, you need to act natural too.'

'This will only be for an evening, Eli. Then we'll get Darcy back home,' Bella added, hoping to calm him down.

Relishing her new fairy disguise, Darcy seemed to grow in confidence. She spoke calmly to Eli, hoping to distract him. 'I noticed you have a beautiful collection of buttons on your bedside table. I was wondering if you'd like another one to add to it?'

Darcy's distraction worked. Eli stopped in his tracks and rushed over to her excitedly. To his delight, Darcy handed him a small silver button plucked from her pyjamas, which he proudly added to his collection.

Across the other side of the bedroom, Felix finished preening his hair in front of the mirror until he was happy it was perfectly coiffed and showing off his lightning-bolt-shaped silver streak. The friends then waited for sunset to leave for the wish wielding arena. Despite the risk of getting caught smuggling a human, they were in high spirits and ready for adventure. Darcy felt a welcome glimmer of magic inside that she hadn't felt for a long time. She held onto it tightly.

Chapter Thirteen

It was a crisp autumn evening and as twilight faded, the sky darkened to a rich, inky blue. In the distance, the friends could see a huge arena, illuminated by beacons of fireflies and twinkling stars overhead. The buzz of excitement from the arena spilled down the hill below, echoing through the valley in anticipation. The friends carefully followed the noise up the narrow gravel path that snaked along the outskirts of the academy, framed by a dark and mysterious forest. Like all fairies, they too had heard stories of the magical forest and the mythical creatures that lived there. Although it was technically owned by the academy, all fairies knew that the natural world could never be claimed. The forest and its inhabitants were tended to by the dedicated academy staff. It was considered a privilege and it made Marta think fondly of Neptune.

As the trail climbed higher and higher towards the arena, it eventually joined a main street, bustling with activity. Fairies, pixies and elves from all backgrounds flooded the streets with colour and cheer. Each of them proudly wearing jerseys and scarves in the colours of their favourite wish wielders, which could also be purchased from various stalls lining the street. Bella, Darcy, Felix and Eli gasped in amazement, blown away by what they saw.

'Wish wielding is big business,' explained Marta.

All around, large neon signs illuminated market stalls, tempting visitors in towards various selections of merchandise, candy floss, nectar fizz and fresh slices of honey pie. A group of young tooth fairies passed by next to them, scoffing down handfuls of toffee, fudge and honeycomb. Felix's eyes bulged wide like dinner plates. His stomach growled in support as he chuckled. 'It always makes me laugh how much tooth fairies like sugar.'

The walk up to the arena was a feast for the senses, full of bright colours and sweet smells from every direction. There was no shortage on entertainment on offer either. Jugglers, fire breathers and street entertainers of all varieties were scattered along the road. As the group meandered slowly through the crowds, Bella and Marta tucked Darcy between them, keeping her safe.

'This is incredible,' Darcy whispered. 'What's going on over there?' She pointed to a large red-and-gold dome, with a long queue of young fairies lined up in front. It looked like a merry-go-round, but with several horse-like creatures inside. Their outlines shone like silver.

'They're unicorns, Darcy,' replied Bella. 'That stall is offering unicorn rides for all the young fairies.'

'Unicorns are real too?!' She almost shrieked with excitement. 'That's amazing. I would love to meet one,' she sighed longingly.

'As it happens, I know someone who might be able to help with that,' giggled Marta. 'But first, let's head to the competition. There's much more magic for you to see before we get you home.'

As they got closer to the stadium, the shadow of the large open tent-like structure loomed over them. It was decorated in thick red-and-white stripes, matching the colours of today's competitors. As this was the first time that most of the friends had been to a wish wielding competition, they were shocked at the sheer size and scale of the arena in front of them. It looked huge, but something told them it would seem even bigger once inside, like a whole other world could reside within.

Outside the arena, fresh crowds gathered next to smaller tents, creating a more frantic atmosphere. These particular stalls were manned by large, green-skinned creatures, with ugly warts and the occasional tuft of hair protruding from their pointy ears and chins.

'Goblins,' whispered Eli to Darcy, as if to answer her silent question.

'And not ones to get noticed by,' added Felix, steering them away from the main queue.

'Why not?' asked Darcy, curiously.

'These goblins are taking bets on who will win tonight,' Marta explained. 'You can bet whatever you like with them. Gold coins, prized possessions, magical potions, even wishes; but the trouble is, goblins never play fair and they hate losing. They will always find a way to pay you back, and then some, so they should never fully be trusted.'

Goblin shouts screeched over the crowd, enticing eager fairies in to gamble.

'Odds on Mirabel,' yelled one. 'Feed your vices for our great prices.'

'Trade for Trixie,' bellowed another. 'It'll only cost your biggest secret.'

Felix shuddered. 'Are they talking about tonight's competitors?'

'Yeah, that's right. Tonight is a battle between highly skilled final-year students, Mirabel Dawn and Trixie Dewdance,' responded Marta. 'Everyone reckons Mirabel is a sure bet to win this evening. She is the first white-cloaked wish wielder in over a century and rumoured to finish top of her class and even take over from Principal Featherstone in the future.'

Darcy looked confused. 'What's so special about having a white cloak?'

Eli grinned smugly, loving the opportunity to show off his knowledge. 'White-cloaked fairies are the rarest types of all. Their magic combines all colours of the rainbow so is more potent than a single colour alone.'

'Almost impossible to stand against,' confirmed Felix, steering them clear of the goblin stalls and through the arched entrance in front of them. As the excitement around grew, the friends hurried up the rows of bleachers above, quick to find their seats for the show.

Finally seated, the friends gasped at the view in front of them. A vast meadow lit by huge lanterns of fireflies scattered and floating magically high above the crowd. In the centre of the meadow stood two metallic podiums that stretched into the sky above, each one adorned with the colours of tonight's competitors. The scene was intimidating. Vast, empty, and undoubtedly a picture of calm before the storm.

From their well-positioned seats, the friends could see thousands of fans streaming into the large arena, increasing the audience size by the minute. They squinted over to the adjoining stand, noticing the royal box, where the most senior and privileged fairies would pay a handsome price to watch the match. Bella rolled her eyes. She suspected that's where Scarlett, Stella and their fortunate families would be watching from.

'Who is that?' exclaimed Darcy, pointing over to a grand-looking fairy in a voluminous lilac dress.

'That is our queen, Darcy,' Marta whispered back. 'Isn't she magnificent?' They both swooned.

'She's up there in the royal box, along with the Fairy Council,' added Eli. 'If you look closely, you can just about make out the silver cloak of Aelfric Albion, Elder of the Elves. He loves a good wish wielding competition, just like all of us elves. Isn't that right, sis?' Eli winked over at his sister.

Halting the hum of conversations through the crowd, a confident voice boomed around the arena, signalling the competition was nearly ready to begin.

'Our majestic queen, fairy folk, and other creatures of the realm, I bid you welcome,' announced Professor Evangeline Joy, renowned wish wielder and referee for this evening. 'Thank you for joining us for what is sure to be an exceptional wish wielding competition, featuring two of my top students.'

The crowd erupted in loud cheers. Professor Joy loved evenings like this, full of energy and theatre. Enjoying the attention from the crowd, she spun dramatically, twirling her emerald green cloak behind her and holding a hand to her ear to encourage the crowd to shout even louder. Her fans gleefully obliged.

On the Professor's cue, loud music started to boom through the speakers around the arena. 'It is now my pleasure to introduce… Your competitors for this evening… Please give a warm welcome to… Mirabel Dawn…. And Trixie Dewdance.'

The crowd's cheers grew to a crescendo as spotlights fell onto each of the metal podiums, revealing a confident but calm, white-cloaked Mirabel, and feisty Trixie, dressed in bright red. They each waved to the crowd, absorbed in the spectacle of the show. After years of hard work and studying at the academy, it was a true privilege for them to be there, performing for the realm.

Professor Joy smiled proudly at her students. 'As you know, points will be awarded for style, skill and magical execution. First to 12 points, wins. As always, I will not tolerate malicious magic, so keep it clean. Remember, this is your final competition before graduation, so don't injure each other, and most importantly, have fun.' She winked in encouragement at Mirabel and Trixie, who each nodded back to signal they were ready.

Adrenalin fizzed round the crowd. Professor Joy held her wand high above her head, pointing up to the stars above. As the music faded and the crowd hushed, an eery silence fell over the arena.

'On my mark, let's begin,' the Professor quietly instructed her students. After a moment, she fired a single streak of green magic, like a beam of light, high into the sky overhead.

The silence was suddenly shattered as Trixie took the first shot. She raised her wand and fired a thin laser of red magic directly at Mirabel, who quickly dived out of the way to avoid the sizzling beam. A chorus of 'ooohs' and 'ahhhs' could be heard around the stadium as the crowd waited for Mirabel's retaliation.

Mirabel leapt from the podium, expanding her wings to take flight. Her translucent wings were edged delicately in white, the same colour as her magic. They glimmered under the moonlight, making Darcy gasp. 'Do all fairies have wings like that?' she whispered to Marta.

'Yes. We all have wings with elements of our magical colours,' Marta replied. 'We can choose to show them whenever we want in this realm, which can be quite handy for flying short distances. But most of the time we keep them hidden for ease, so we're not knocking things over. Pretty cool, huh?' Darcy nodded in amazement, staring back at the competition in front of her.

From her new vantage point, Mirabel could now easily take aim at Trixie. She fired back a bright white lasso of light, trying to trap Trixie within its grasp. The lasso fizzed with electricity as it shot towards Trixie like lightning.

In a surprise movement, Trixie leapt up towards the lasso, spreading her red-tipped wings as she flew into the air. From her wand, she cast a defensive red billow of smoke. The explosion of colour temporarily stunned Mirabel's lasso, giving Trixie a moment to avoid it. She fired back a piercing shot that crackled faintly as it grazed the tip of Mirabel's wing.

This was a close competition, there was no denying it. The crowd responded gleefully with loud cheers as Professor Joy awarded the first point to Trixie. She clapped in encouragement, willing both of her students to continue.

Mirabel seemed frustrated. She felt a great weight on her shoulders as a white-cloaked fairy godmother and didn't want to let anyone down. She summoned all the power she could muster, sending bright white light erupting from the tip of her wand. As the strike flew, it took on the form of a dragon, breathing white fire as it shot forwards angrily. Trixie didn't have long to react.

Seeing the immediate threat fast approaching, she tried desperately to conjure a shield to defend herself against the magical flames but was not quick or strong enough against Mirabel's powerful magic. The flames knocked Trixie from her podium, giving a clear point back to Mirabel. The crowd roared in response.

The duel continued as Mirabel and Trixie twisted and dived, filling the night's sky with colourful clouds of fluorescent magic. These wish wielding competitions only ever happened on a full moon, because the Fairy Council worried that the huge amounts of light may even be seen from the human realm. The same thought crossed Darcy's mind too. To her, the magic danced across the sky like the Northern Lights.

Continuing strong, Mirabel took aim again at Trixie. This time, her attack took the form of a wild unicorn. Its bright white light charged across the open air, stampeding horn first towards Trixie's podium. Although Trixie's magic was weaker than Mirabel's, she was more cunning and determined. She conjured up her own magical lasso and flung it towards the white unicorn, catching its horn to throw it off course. In the same instant, Trixie fired back a bright red arrow that hurtled towards Mirabel's head. The crowd gasped, on the edge of their seats at the skilful display overhead.

With the battle well underway, Bella nudged Marta to signal it was time to leave. Darcy was so in awe of the wondrous magic she was witnessing that she could barely tear her eyes away. She knew she would dream about this and hoped one day she would also be able to tell her children about it too, just like the treasured stories her mother had told her.

As discreetly as possible, the friends stood from their seats, using the ongoing spectacle as the diversion they needed to make their escape. They crept back down towards the exit, passing through the surrounding crowd unnoticed – exactly the cover they needed to get back to the library. It was time to get Darcy home.

Chapter Fourteen

The friends headed hastily back towards the main entrance of the arena. With the battle raging above, the lobby was fairly empty, except for a few straggling spectators and more hungry tooth fairies looking for a snack. Much to Darcy's surprise, the air around the arena no longer smelt sweet. It was instead filled with the scent of lingering smoke and crackling fire. Much like after a bonfire.

As the friends checked to make sure the coast was clear, ready to make their final escape into the night, they were stopped in their tracks by a familiar voice.

'Good evening, students,' greeted the authoritative voice, in an unusually cheerful manner.

They turned to see the familiar face of Professor Curtis, with an unfamiliar flush to his cheeks.

'Good evening, Professor,' replied Felix, keen to keep the conversation as short as possible.

'Are you enjoying the show?' the Professor asked, surveying his group of students.

'Very much so,' nodded Eli eagerly. Eli was not normally very good at lying, but luckily on this occasion,

Professor Curtis didn't seem to notice. 'We just came down here to find a snack.'

'Good idea, my boy!' Professor Curtis slapped Eli on the back enthusiastically. 'Sustenance is key for an event like this! I myself have come down here for another glass of dandelion spritz. Just don't tell Principal Featherstone.' He gave Eli a conspiratorial wink. He was most definitely tipsy.

The friends let out a forced laughed, unsure how to fill the awkward silence that followed. Professor Curtis seemed unfazed. Until he noticed something strange. His gaze landed uncomfortably on Darcy.

'I don't believe we've met… Are you a new student?' he asked her directly.

Darcy, hoping to remain unnoticed, spluttered in shock, quickly covering it up with a cough.

Marta, who was naturally a much better liar than her brother, answered for her. 'Yeah, this is Darcy. She's just started at the academy, so we're showing her round.' Darcy gave a shy smile that she hoped looked credible enough.

Professor Curtis nodded thoughtfully, looking her up and down. His eyes locked onto her treasured pendant. 'My, my, my… That is a beautiful gemstone, Darcy. It reminds me of the old and powerful crystals we used to ship in from ancient magic mine.' He paused to admire the pendant some more. 'I myself have never been lucky enough to possess one, but I am told they have magical properties.' He arched an eyebrow. 'A splendid and no doubt very valuable family heirloom indeed,' he added, eyes awkwardly transfixed on the gem and practically salivating.

'Thank you,' squeaked Darcy, embarrassed by the unwanted attention and unsure how to respond.

More cheers for Mirabel erupted loudly overhead, prompting Professor Curtis to snap out of his trance. 'Well, I must be off, students. My hip flask won't refill itself.' He continued merrily, 'Have a good evening and a very warm welcome again, Darcy. You're lucky to have these lot looking after you.' With a final flamboyant swish of his purple cloak, Professor Curtis tottered off in the direction of the nearest beverage stall.

'Well, that was excruciating,' said Marta, trying to physically shake off the awkwardness from their encounter.

Bella agreed. 'Very uncomfortable. Are you okay, Darcy?'

Darcy nodded with a grimace. 'I'm fine. But are all your teachers seriously that weird?'

The friends burst out laughing. 'Fortunately not,' chuckled Felix. 'And with any luck, Professor Curtis was so merry he won't remember a thing about that tomorrow.'

'He might have a bit of a headache though,' added Eli, shaking his head in second-hand embarrassment.

Something else about the encounter with Professor Curtis also niggled at Bella's mind. She pondered out loud, 'If Darcy's gem really is from the ancient magic mine, then maybe that's where we need to go?'

'My thoughts exactly,' agreed Marta. 'It's literally the birthplace of fairy magic, so if it has something to do with how she got here in the first place, maybe it will hold the clue to get her back home too.'

'It's very dangerous though, and not to mention, across the other side of the realm and surrounded by goblins,' argued Eli. Suddenly self-conscious and not wanting to sound too negative, he added tentatively, 'But I'm sure it's nothing that we can't handle together.'

Felix smiled at his best friend, adding what was clearly on the tip of Eli's tongue. 'No harm in doing some research first so we know what we're up against.' Eli smiled back, letting out a long sigh of relief.

'You're right. We don't even know how to get there to begin with,' huffed Bella. 'Let's head back to the library to investigate.'

The friends continued on with fresh urgency, now keener than ever to leave the arena. They hurried out of the stadium onto the main street, which was now mostly deserted. The only exceptions were a few remaining goblin stalls. The goblins glared at them, searching hungrily for any signs of desperation they could prey upon.

'That's a pretty necklace you have there, my dear,' shouted one to Darcy.

'How much is it worth to you?' heckled another.

Bella steered Darcy away quickly before they could harass her anymore. 'Which way now?' she asked.

'You're not going to like this, Eli,' Marta replied, turning to look directly at her nervous younger brother. 'The quickest way back is through the forest.'

The friends stood timidly in a line at the edge of the forest, staring into the dark abyss that greeted them. They didn't know exactly what was in the forest, but they did know it was not a safe place to wander alone. Especially at night. Especially without a map.

They knew the forest was home to many magical creatures, some friendly and others not. Although they couldn't be sure, it left them with the distinct feeling that they were being watched. Wind howled through the overhanging branches, whistling a warning. Through the distant darkness, Eli thought he could make out several pairs of small glowing yellow eyes. By the time he had blinked, they had disappeared. Eli wished they could go back to the bright lights and relative safety of the arena. He'd sooner try his luck there with the goblins than scramble through the forest.

'This is one of the stupidest ideas you've ever had, sis,' groaned Eli.

'I know this looks bad,' began Marta, 'but this is by far the quickest way back to the academy.' Sensing the rest of her friends were also unsure, she continued on optimistically, 'Besides, Neptune is working tonight, so all we need to do is find him and he'll show us the rest of the way.'

'Even I'm not sure about this,' conceded Bella. Felix remained quiet, signalling his agreement by staring down at the ground and scuffing his trainers on the dirt.

'I know it looks scary,' acknowledged Darcy naively, 'but surely we'll be okay if we all stick together?'

Marta gave Darcy a big squeeze, grateful for her support. The fairy disguise certainly agreed with her confidence.

'Exactly,' agreed Marta. 'We know that Neptune is looking after the unicorns tonight, and we know that the main stables are not far from the arena...'

'Unicorns!' interrupted Darcy excitedly. 'Please, can we try to find them?' She practically begged her new friends.

Bella chuckled, feeling torn between trying to keep Darcy safe, and also wanting to make her happy. She thought of a compromise that everyone might agree to. 'Okay, so how about we have a quick look near here for Neptune? If we don't find him, we'll be close enough to the edge of the forest to find the gravel path again and follow it back the long way to the library? Does that sound like a plan?'

The friends nodded. Taking one last look at the bright lights of the arena behind them, they turned towards the dark forest and walked nervously in. Bella and Marta led the way, keeping Darcy safe behind them. Eli followed closely, with Felix on lookout from behind.

As they walked further into the forest, darkness closed around them until they could no longer see the bright lights from the arena. Instead, they followed a narrow dirt path through the forest, lined each side by thick brambles. The air smelt damp and heavy. There was little to see or hear, except for the crunching of leaves and snapping of twigs as they continued slowly forwards. In the distance, they could hear the faint calls and howls of unknown creatures, but fortunately these seemed far away.

Noticing something strange happening to her gemstone pendant, Darcy suddenly gasped.

'Are you okay, Darcy?' asked Bella urgently, unsure what was wrong. She turned round to face Darcy, immediately noticing her gemstone was glowing, flashing sporadically with bright turquoise light.

'Has your necklace ever done that before?' asked Marta.

Darcy shook her head in denial. She had always believed her gemstone was special. After all, her mother had told her so. But even she was surprised to see it glowing in front of her, as if by magic.

A pair of magpies screeched overhead, squawking aggressively from their perch. The friends could now hear deep voices in the distance. They seemed to be getting closer by the second.

'Quick, hide,' hissed Bella. They scrambled behind two large trees, squatting down for cover as the voices grew closer.

Peeking out through the brambles, they could now see a pair of large goblins stomping past. They looked like the goblins they had seen earlier running the gambling tents outside the arena. This time, they wheeled heavy wooden carts behind them, laden with trinkets and magical artefacts. Their prizes from tonight. The goblins gloated to each other, too busy boasting about their winnings to notice the friends hiding in the bushes. Before long, they had passed, leaving the path safe again for the friends to continue. They all breathed a sigh of relief.

'That was close,' exhaled Felix.

Bella agreed. She looked round at Darcy to check she was okay. 'Your necklace has stopped glowing now,' she observed. 'I think your mother was right, it really must be a protective charm.'

'Whatever it was,' added Marta, 'we're grateful it saved us. That could have turned out really badly if we'd have been caught.'

Darcy smiled, finally starting to feel like she'd found somewhere she belonged. A shimmer of gold caught her eye on the path up ahead. 'What's that on the ground? It looks like some kind of scroll?'

Eli walked over to pick it up. 'Well, here's another stroke of good luck. It's a map. It must have fallen out of one of the goblin's carts,' he beamed, unrolling the gold-edged scroll. 'And by the look of things, it's a magical elvish map.'

Before Darcy could ask what made this so special, Eli explained, 'Elvish maps are known to be the most detailed of all maps in our realm. They are always accurate because the magic used to draw them means they always stay up to date. Watch this.'

Darcy watched as Eli slowly turned with the map, moving to face each direction of the compass. As he did so, the map magically changed, as if scanning the surrounding forest like a radar and translating it onto the page in front of them in bright scrawling illustrations. Darcy was amazed.

With new-found confidence, Eli now took the lead. 'We'll find Neptune in no time with this.'

The friends followed closely behind him as he skilfully navigated the maze-like forest, avoiding a series of dead ends and sharp drops that may have otherwise claimed them.

Before long, they saw light up ahead in the distance that looked like a woodland clearing. As they approached, the forest opened wide to reveal a large field of lush green grass. The friends could finally see the sky again and stared up to admire the stars. Eli smiled smugly.

In the middle of the field was a large wooden stable. Marta could just about see the outline of a tall, cloaked figure she recognised. They'd found Neptune.

Chapter Fifteen

'Neptune!' Marta called fondly as the friends rushed over to the stables. Breaching the inner part of the forest was like stepping into another world altogether. The field was truly an oasis in the middle of the dim and mysterious woodland. Bright green and plush, like a freshly laid carpet, it was clear it had been tended to with great care and pride. Starlight twinkled overhead, bathing the clearing in bright silver light. For the first time since entering the forest, the friends felt safe again.

Hearing his name, Neptune spun round on the spot. He was delighted to see Marta and her friends, if not a little surprised too. 'What are you all doing here?' he asked, smiling directly at Marta. Then noticing Darcy, he added warmly, 'And who's this?'

Before answering, Marta flung her arms round his neck, filled with an overwhelming sense of relief at seeing him. She pulled him tightly into an unexpected hug. 'It's really good to see you Neptune.' When she finally released him, they were both blushing, grinning widely at each other.

Bella coughed awkwardly to regain their attention. 'This is Darcy,' Bella answered, bringing the meeting back to business. 'It's a bit of a long story, but we need to get to the library urgently to find a way to get her home.'

'Well, it's nice to meet you, Darcy.' Neptune released his gaze from Marta with ever so slight reluctance, to shake Darcy's hand. 'I'd be happy to help. What do you need?'

'We were hoping you might be able to show us the quickest way back to the library from here,' said Marta, batting her lashes. 'And perhaps let us borrow a couple of unicorns to fly there?'

Neptune pondered the request for a moment, before Darcy interrupted. 'Do you really have real-life unicorns here?' she asked, unable to hide her wide-eyed excitement at the prospect.

Neptune chuckled. 'Yes, we do, and I am very proud to look after them. I don't suppose you would like to meet them?'

Darcy squealed in reply.

'I'll take that as a yes,' Neptune laughed. Growing up in the magical realm, he had never met someone who had never seen an actual unicorn before, let alone a human who didn't know of their existence. It reminded him of how he felt when he first quit his studies at the academy, dropping out of his second year to take on a caretaker position, much to the bewilderment of his peers. It was a big decision to make, but an opportunity he couldn't pass up. He had always loved working with animals and being out in nature. He remembered with great fondness and tenderness how wondrous everything felt at first. The first time he flew a unicorn. The first time he met a griffin. He felt it was truly his calling and relished the opportunity to show off his work to Marta and her friends. It was endearing.

As he walked over to the stable door, he gestured for the friends to follow. As Darcy was learning, along with most things in this realm, the stable also seemed to be much bigger on the inside than it looked from the exterior. Despite its large area, it still managed to feel cosy. Wooden beams were illuminated by strings of firefly lights that cast a charming warm glow across the length of the barn. Within the stable were three individual pens for each of the unicorns. As Neptune entered, the unicorns neighed, enthusiastically greeting their friend.

Neptune led Darcy and the others over to the first pen. At its entrance was a large mahogany half-gate decorated with a cascade of small pearls that stretched from floor to ceiling. The pattern was beautifully detailed and painfully precise. Darcy thought it must have taken hours.

'Each of the unicorns has their own personality, just like us, so we try to decorate their homes to match,' explained Neptune. As if approving of Neptune's explanation, a young-looking unicorn poked its head over the gate to examine their guests. It had a bright white coat, framed by a delicately plaited silver mane that was also interwoven with small pearls.

'Darcy, this is Snowdrop,' Neptune continued. 'As you can tell, she likes to be well groomed. Feel free to say hello, just avoid her horn unless she invites you to touch it.'

Slightly apprehensively, Darcy approached the gate. 'Hello, Snowdrop,' she said softly, extending her hand towards the unicorn to examine. After a brief sniff, Snowdrop licked Darcy's hand in approval and lowered her head to be petted.

'She likes you,' praised Neptune. 'Unicorns are usually a very good judge of character.'

Darcy was elated and continued to pet Snowdrop, tickling her muzzle. 'You're so beautiful, Snowdrop.' The unicorn replied with a short neigh as if to agree. Darcy had always loved horses and thought they were the most emotionally intelligent creatures she had ever seen. Yet, being with the unicorns was even more magical. They had a silent wisdom and powerful stare that Darcy could swear could see into a person's soul. She felt an instant bond with Snowdrop.

Neptune walked over to the neighbouring gate to introduce his second unicorn, Onyx. Again, this stable was decorated differently, painted in a rich black paint that shimmered iridescently under the warm light. There was no other decoration of note and nothing fancy adorning the pen. This unicorn was content with a simple magical shimmer. Neptune peeked over the top of the gate and gave it three strong knocks to entice Onyx over. 'Onyx, here boy, come out and say hello to our guests.'

A moment later, the friends were greeted by a majestic stallion of a unicorn. Onyx stood proudly with a deep black coat. His horn shimmered with all the colours of the rainbow, matching the rich paint that decorated his pen. He gave a gentle bow of his head in greeting, before turning back to munch on a large bale of hay hanging to the side of his gate.

'Unicorns are so cool,' exclaimed Darcy.

Neptune smiled proudly. 'They are. But Marta and Bella have cool pets too,' he continued, walking over to the final stable. 'Marta's pet hedgehog, Luna, has spines that can make her invisible, and Bella's snail, Dorothy, has a special slime that glows in the dark.'

'Does she really?' exclaimed Bella. 'I never knew that.'

'Oh yes,' replied Neptune. 'A jar of Dorothy's slime would be at least ten times brighter than a jar of fireflies.'

Bella nodded, impressed by this new-found information. Neptune's knowledge about creatures of the magical realm was second to none. He clearly cared a great deal about his work looking after the animals and grounds. Bella had grown to like him a lot. He was gentle and sweet-natured and seemed to make her friend Marta very happy, which is what she cared about most of all.

'This is all so wonderful,' beamed Darcy in disbelief, still trying to take in her magical surroundings. The group moved to the final pen, which had an entrance gate decorated with clusters of platinum roses, surrounded by sharp, gold, metallic thorns. A beautiful dappled grey and white unicorn approached from within.

'And finally,' explained Neptune, 'this is Sparkles.'

Seeming to take note of Neptune's proximity to Marta, Sparkles let out a long huff through slightly flared nostrils, signalling her mild annoyance. Neptune laughed awkwardly. 'Sorry, she wasn't exactly named for her sparkling personality. Ironic really. She can be a bit moody and I think she might be a bit jealous of you, Marta.' Embarrassed, he added, 'I might happen to talk about you rather a lot.' He scuffed his boots shyly along the floor.

Marta blushed again, but this time she was determined to stay on track with their plan. 'Well, this has been amazing, thanks Neptune, but we really should get moving if we're going to make it back to the library before sunrise.'

'Of course,' replied Neptune dutifully, 'I'll get these lot saddled up.' Turning back to his unicorns, he added, 'Fancy a night flight?' They all neighed happily in reply.

Once saddled, Neptune helped Eli and Felix onto Onyx, and Bella and Darcy onto their favourite unicorn, Snowdrop. Darcy nuzzled into Snowdrop's mane, who let out a small trill of happiness in response. When finally ready, Neptune climbed onto a reluctant Sparkles and hoisted an equally anxious Marta up behind him. With Sparkles leading the way at the front, flanked each side by Snowdrop and Onyx, the unicorns left the stable and trotted across to the far edge of the field, ready to take flight.

'Now, whatever you do, hold on tight,' shouted Neptune to the others. The instructions were brief but felt urgent enough to take note of. The friends complied, gripping tightly onto their reins as the unicorns began to canter in formation. They ran quicker and quicker until eventually breaking into a full gallop across the vast field, hurtling towards the trees in front of them. As they reached the very edge of the forest, with one forceful push from the ground, the unicorns launched themselves vertically upwards against the tree-line, spreading their wings wide and taking flight towards the stars overhead. After clearing the trees, the unicorns stabilised, soaring high through the sky towards the horizon. The cold air rushed against the friends' faces, making them feel more alive than ever as they admired the beauty of the realm below.

'This is amazing,' cheered Darcy, 'I feel like I'm on top of the world.'

Sensing her enjoyment, Snowdrop twisted and turned through the air, making Darcy feel like she was on a rollercoaster. Before long, Onyx and Sparkles joined in too, not wanting to miss out on all the fun. The herd swooped and swerved through the night sky until finally tired of playing. They glided on peacefully over the wide canopy of trees below, heading towards the outline of the academy that loomed in the distance.

Chapter Sixteen

In a perfectly choreographed manoeuvre, the group touched down beside the library, landing gently on the grass bank outside. The friends hopped off, patting their unicorns gratefully. All except Marta, who was just relieved to have dismounted her moody unicorn and maintained a cautious distance from Sparkles at all times. Darcy hugged Snowdrop's neck and gave her a big kiss on her muzzle.

Marta turned to Neptune. 'Thank you, for everything.' She gave him a gentle peck on the cheek, turning his face an obvious shade of bright pink.

Neptune smiled back. 'You're welcome Marta. I hope you find what you're looking for in there.' Although he would have loved to have spent more time with Marta, sailing through the night's sky, he didn't want to hold them up any longer. He leapt confidently onto Sparkles' back looking every bit the hero, while skilfully grabbing the reins for Onyx and Snowdrop too. 'And it was lovely to meet you, Darcy.' With a final wave, Neptune and the unicorns galloped into the distance, launching back into the sky towards the forest from whence they came.

'Well, what did you think of that then, Darcy?' asked Felix cheerfully.

'That was by far the best thing I have ever done in my life!' replied Darcy, watching the unicorns shrink as they soared further into the distance and eventually out of sight altogether.

Bella laughed. 'We're pleased to hear. Now, let's get into that library and find a way to get you home.'

Eli glanced over at Darcy's necklace. 'Assuming your gemstone really does come from the ancient magic mine like Professor Curtis said, the mine will probably hold the clue we're looking for. I suggest we start looking there,' he added studiously.

Marta nodded. 'And it will be much easier this time, because anything to do with realm history will be in the main section of the library. We'll just need to find it.'

Under the cover of moonlight, the friends crept through the side door of the library. The door seemed as old as time, rotting and creaky, covered in moss. It looked like a secret entrance, long forgotten. As Marta pushed it open, it groaned loudly in disapproval, making her worry that others might hear them. Thankfully, as the friends stepped through the threshold into the main library, it appeared to be empty, except for the high shelves stretching in either direction and the familiar musty smell of old books. It seemed like the whole realm was out, no doubt still enthralled at the wish wielding competition back up at the arena. The friends felt confident in their plan.

'Right, team, get to it,' bossed Bella. 'Darcy and I will take this row. Marta, you take the row by the fireplace, and boys, you take the row by the study benches. Let us know as soon as you find anything to do with the ancient mine.'

The friends split up and began scouring the rows of books for anything useful that might tell them more about the history of the ancient magic mine and Darcy's gemstone. While searching on the far side of the library, Felix thought he heard a strange noise. He paused his search, straining to hear the faint but unnerving sound.

'Did you hear that, Eli?' he asked furtively. 'It sounded like someone was whispering.'

Eli shook his head, making Felix assume he must have imagined the noise, until the mysterious whispers came again, this time louder. Eli gave Felix a nervous look, letting him know that this time he'd heard them too. They seemed to be coming from the other side of the book shelf. They didn't know who else would be here at this time of night, so they proceeded cautiously.

'Hello?' called Felix towards the shelf in front of them. 'Who's there?'

The mysterious whispers suddenly stopped.

Felix was not one to be easily spooked. He grabbed hold of a nervous Eli and dragged him roughly along to the end of the row to investigate. As soon as they turned the corner towards the study desks, Felix and Eli were surprised to see they weren't alone in the library as they had first thought. A startled Tempest and Talia Summersong stared back at them from behind their glass study lamps, with furrowed brows and wide hazel eyes. Eli and Felix relaxed again.

'Phew,' exhaled Felix. 'It's just you two.'

'What are you doing here?' Eli asked the twins, eyeing them suspiciously.

'We didn't fancy going to the wish wielding competition,' replied Tempest, staring back at him with equal scepticism. 'It's just not really our thing.'

Hearing the commotion, Bella, Marta and Darcy burst round the corner to check on their friends.

Despite the clever disguise, Talia spotted Darcy instantly. She was known to be quieter and more perceptive than her twin sister and stared at Darcy in open-mouthed fascination.

'Sh-she's a human! W-what is she doing—' Talia stopped abruptly before she could finish her sentence. She glanced back at her sister Tempest, deep in thought. Although to the outside world it seemed like they were staring silently at each other, the twins were used to using their telepathic connection to communicate privately. They mostly used this strange skill to gossip or secretly plan how to annoy their older brother, Neptune, but it also came in handy for moments like this when they needed to confer.

When they'd finished their secret discussion, Talia continued, 'Actually, on second thought, don't answer that. We don't want to know what trouble you've got yourselves into and we don't want any part of it.' The twins flicked their long auburn hair in dismissal.

Still hoping for their help, Bella pleaded, 'We're just here to find out about the ancient magic mine and then we'll be out of here, we promise. Do you know where we can find anything about it?'

The twins paused again in consideration. This time Tempest replied, 'Well, that should be easy enough.' She walked over to the nearest bookshelf and pulled down a heavy, green, leather-bound volume. 'This book is all about the history of the ancient mine. It's one of our favourites.' The friends sat down as Tempest opened the cover and began to read to the group.

'*Once upon a time, when our realm was young, all magical creatures lived here in peace and harmony. Every creature knew their role and worked together to maintain balance with the natural world, never taking more than nature intended and replenishing the land's resources. During this time, our fairy magic was fuelled by fairy dust from the ancient magic mine.*' As she read, technicolour holograms burst forward from the book, projecting the story into a floating iridescent bubble in front of them. It was as if the book itself was dreaming, immersing its audience in bright images and vivid visions of time gone by.

'*The mine was tended to by goblins, whose job it was to gather and supply fairy dust for the fairies of the realm. Over time, the goblins grew bitter and frustrated, angry that they controlled the supply of fairy dust, yet had no magic themselves. They became obsessed. Determined to take over the realm and overthrow the queen. As the goblin army grew in strength, they were joined by a white-cloaked fairy godmother who was sympathetic to their cause. Equally power hungry, but far more powerful, she became their leader. But she was driven slowly insane by her desire to rule the realm. Over time, tension grew throughout the land until it fatefully erupted. Friends became foes. Allies became enemies. Our realm succumbed to battle…'* Tempest turned the page as the friends hung on her every word.

'After several agonising conflicts throughout the realm, it became clear that action was needed to end the war once and for all and prevent fairy folk from being overthrown. All fairies of our realm, from all backgrounds, were called upon by our queen to work together to end the war. By combining their magic through a shared dream cast, they had the collective power needed to defeat the goblin army. But it came at great cost. The land was scarred from war and our oldest oak tree was destroyed. To this day, The Goblin War remains our greatest shame. Yet, this tale is one of triumph, not sorrow. For even in the darkest times, there is always hope. From the ashes, grew our treasured toadstool, which has since become our main source of magic. The mine was abandoned and the remaining goblins were defeated and went into hiding. Our prestigious Fairy Council was created to ensure balance remained in the realm and that a tragedy like this would never happen again.'

When Tempest had finished, she closed the book with a flourish. The story had left a sombre atmosphere in the room as Bella and her friends realised exactly what could be at stake if the toadstool's powers were not restored. Without a stable supply of magic, the realm may once again descend into war. Let alone what could happen to humanity. If fairies lost their magic, there would be no one left to protect humankind. The result could be devastating.

'Would you mind if I borrowed that?' asked Eli, pointing towards the book in Tempest's hands.

'Sure,' she replied, handing him the thick, leather-covered book. Eli cradled it delicately over to the fireplace and continued reading, enthralled by the stories it held. His friends joined him on the plush sofas, ready to plot their next move.

'This is fascinating,' exclaimed Eli, barely able to tear his eyes away from the pages in front of him.' There's also a section in here about gemstones from the mine. They look a lot like Darcy's.'

As he turned the page and read out loud, colourful diagrams sprung to life before their eyes. '*Gemstones from the ancient magic mine are some of the most precious and rarest of our realm. Forged in darkness, under tremendous pressure, they contain potentially unlimited amounts of pure magic. Each with its own unique charm, they are full of raw power that can be manipulated by the owner for their own intent. Some gemstones are known to have powers of protection. While others may be powerful enough to allow the wearer to jump between our land and the human realm, without a portal. There are still many things we don't know about these gemstones and it is possible we will never unlock all of their mysteries, but one thing is certain, combining the magic of the stones would create a power the likes of which the realm has never known…'*

As Eli read, a near perfect replica of Darcy's gemstone floated off the page and shimmered in front of them. It spun in the air, suspended in time and flitting between bright turquoise and soft purple, just like the real thing. It was almost as if Darcy could reach out and touch it. She imagined it too would feel cool to touch, with rough edges, just like the gemstone that hung around her neck.

'The mine really might hold the key to getting Darcy home then, if that's where her gemstone is from,' summarised Bella.

'And if these gemstones are as powerful as the book says they are, they might also be able to help restore the realm's magic,' agreed Marta, before explaining their encounter with the Fairy Council to Darcy.

After a moment's thought, Darcy replied selflessly, 'Then that's where we must go. If there's any chance we can fix things, we must at least try. The human world needs fairy magic now more than ever.'

Chapter Seventeen

The friends gathered nervously by the entrance to the library. Huddled under the soft glow of firefly lamps, they felt safe and warm. But they knew this would soon change if they ventured through unknown parts of their realm to the ancient mine. They didn't know much about what existed in these areas of their world, but they did expect it would be dangerous. They also knew they didn't have long to make their escape. It would soon be sunrise, and with the wish wielding competition finished, the academy would once again be swarming with fairies. If they stayed much longer, it would be harder to sneak away, and even harder to keep Darcy's presence a secret. They had to make their move, and they had to make it now.

Eli clutched the enchanted history book tightly to his chest like a comfort blanket. 'This could be very dangerous,' worried Eli as he considered their plan, or lack thereof.

'You're right, Eli, but there must be something we can do to turn the odds more in our favour?' asked Felix tenaciously.

'We're lucky to have Darcy and her protection gem,' added Bella. 'That's got to count for something.' She smiled over at Darcy.

'And there might even be more we can do to protect ourselves,' wondered Marta. 'Do you remember what Neptune said in the forest about our pets, Luna and Dorothy?'

'You're a genius, Marta!' Bella beamed as if reading Marta's mind.

'I know,' she replied nonchalantly, but typically failing to keep up the cool facade, broke out into a giggle. Marta continued, 'So, we'll get an invisibility spine from Luna and some glow-in-the-dark slime from Dorothy before we head off.'

Feeling more confident, the friends left the library, heading back through the network of underground corridors towards their dormitory in Kingfisher Hall. Although the corridors were known to be maze-like, Bella and Eli felt certain that after their last visit to the library, they would be able to find their way back without a hitch. They just hoped the corridors would comply with their wish.

'But how will we even get to the mine?' questioned Felix, as they wondered down another dimly lit hallway.

'The quickest way would be to realm jump,' guessed Eli. He knew from the enchanted book he was carrying that the mine was very far away. It would be too far to fly and take too long by any other means, let alone the risk of them getting spotted or caught out in the open. But, if they could realm jump to the edge of the mine, or at least close to it, it would surely be easy enough to find from there. Since they had all performed well in their first realm jumping lesson, Eli felt sure they could do it together.

'It's as good an idea as any we've had so far,' agreed Bella, 'but for that, we'll need some more fairy dust.'

'Luckily, I have plenty of that hidden in our room too,' remembered Marta.

Bella laughed. 'As I said before Marta, you're a genius.'

The friends continued meandering through the cold and damp zigzagging tunnels. Enchanted candles floated mysteriously, framing each side of the rough limestone walls to provide just enough light for the next few steps ahead. It was more than a little unnerving and it was starting to feel like the alleyways were leading them astray.

As they passed each junction of the maze-like corridor, new passageways branched off, seemingly at random towards different parts of the academy. These cryptic turnings were marked by occasional lopsided lamp posts that seemed to appear from thin air. However, as Bella noticed first, these signs had now come to a curious halt. She slowed the group to a gentle walk, trying to regain their bearings.

'This seems to be taking a lot longer than usual,' Bella puzzled.

'Are we lost?' asked Darcy, nervously. She glanced down at her gemstone necklace to make sure it wasn't glowing. Fortunately, it remained its usual purple-blue iridescent hue.

'I hope not,' Bella replied, trying to maintain a sense of calm and composure. Although in truth, she couldn't be sure. The tunnels seemed to have a mind of their own, varying in size, shape and direction like a web of tangled roots searching for water. As if detecting their reluctance, the tunnel sloped spontaneously downwards, edging the friends forward. The sudden change in elevation caused Felix to trip, crashing forward into Eli, also knocking him off balance. With a gasp, the enchanted book fell from Eli's hands and tumbled onto the dark pavement some way in front of them. Its leather covers flew open, sending a cascade of coloured lights scattering across the ceiling of the ever narrowing tunnel.

As Eli rushed to collect the enchanted book, he saw the symphony of lights were not in fact random. The book was projecting visions all around them, as if to guide them. It was like a magical diary, broadcasting the tunnels' memories through centuries past. Glittering gemstones, precious amulets, forbidden spells. All manner of magical objects and enchantments once hidden and long lost within the mysterious tunnels were now displayed as vivid shadows in front of them.

Darcy spotted something that caught her eye in the kaleidoscope of treasures. An age-worn wooden shield, with a simple leather strap. It was so out of place between the sparkling jewels and golden chests that it stuck out immediately. Although she thought others may think it tatty and weathered, she admired its simplicity. It looked sturdy and reliable, like it had survived many a battle. There was an understated nobility to it that she couldn't describe, but she could definitely feel. She reached out to touch it, hoping it would materialise in her hands directly from the image above her.

In that moment, the enchantment was broken. With a rustle of pages, the magical book slammed shut, shattering the visions and plunging the tunnel back into darkness. Before they knew what was happening, the tunnel pinched in behind them, forcing them forward in a single-file line as the corridor closed behind. Eli followed at the rear, scooping the book up from the floor just in time and chasing his friends through the quickly closing cavern. Breathless, they sprinted forwards in the only direction they could, until eventually greeted by a large open space where everything was quiet and still once more. The friends came to a grinding halt and caught their breath, trying to work out where they had been brought to.

It was well known that the tunnels had been built with protection charms that were needed to protect fairy folk during the Goblin War. These charms were typically used to mislead the eye to conceal items of value, or direct travellers to their doom or towards help, depending on their intent. It seemed like these charms were still in full effect. Working in partnership with the magical book, the tunnels had conspired to help the friends in need, bringing them to somewhere or something that would help them. They just needed to work out why.

In contrast to the rugged limestone tunnel, the room they had found themselves in was a cocoon of fresh, white marble. It glimmered around them, making Darcy feel like she was in a posh museum. In the centre of the room was a glass display case, open on one side. Perched proudly in the middle of the display was the same wooden shield that Darcy recognised from the visions she had just seen projected around the tunnel. Darcy walked over to the display case. A simple plaque sat below, with a delicate gold inscription: 'The Shield of Honour'. As she read the plaque, a small scroll fell from the display case down to her feet. She unravelled it and read it to her friends, '*May it protect you fiercely with the strength of platinum, only if your heart is pure. But if you harbour wicked thoughts, may it hold as weak as moss and straw.*'

'I think it wants you to take it, Darcy,' prompted Eli.

'That must be why we've been brought here,' agreed Bella.

'At least it will provide some extra protection for the mine,' added Marta.

As if the shield was calling out to her, Darcy lifted it carefully from the glass cabinet and hooked it over her shoulder, surprised at the weightiness of it. She admired the soft, velvety grain of the leather strap and felt the coarseness of the wood. Should she need it, it would make a very fine shield indeed.

'We should get out of here,' suggested Bella, not wanting to push their luck much further.

Marta agreed. 'It must almost be sunrise, so we better get a move on.'

'Wait,' exclaimed Felix as they gathered by the exit to leave. 'What's that over there?'

He strolled back across the room to a discreet marble shelf that he hadn't noticed before. On it sat a golden lamp, decorated with small chips of multi-coloured crystals that had been polished into a glittering shine.

Felix had no idea if it had been there the whole time or if it had just appeared. The tunnel seemed to work in mysterious ways like that. Regardless, he was captivated. Unable to resist the temptation, he grabbed the lamp and hurried back to the others.

United again, the friends backed out of the gallery, once more in the main corridor. As if satisfied with a job well done, the tunnel had mercifully changed direction again. Up ahead the friends were delighted to finally see a shimmering sign for Kingfisher Hall. They rushed towards it, bursting in through their dormitory door.

Chapter Eighteen

Instantly comforted by the familiar sight of their dormitory, the friends let out a collective sigh of relief. Darcy stared out of the large arched window in the centre of the room, gazing down on the wondrous landscape below. The moon was now setting, sending its last few rays of silver light shimmering across the crystal lake. As the sun teased to rise over the horizon, flecks of deep orange and speckles of gold began to punctuate the fading purple sky. It could not have been more beautiful if it were painted on a canvas.

Darcy hadn't been able to take everything in the last time she was here, after she had crashed abruptly through her dream into the fairy realm. She now took time to cherish every detail. She admired the delicate inscriptions that had been carved across the walls and ceilings. Although she didn't know what they meant, she thought they fitted the room perfectly, adding an enduring quality that she felt all magical things should have. She also admired the brightly polished mahogany furniture. The crystal lamps. The velvet cushions. The soft, textured throws in each of the fairies' colours that decorated their beds. But, above all, she admired the new friends she had found. Nothing made her smile as much as seeing the group of fairies that now surrounded her. Despite the urgency of their mission, she had not felt this at peace in years.

'Would you like to meet Luna and Dorothy?' asked Marta, beginning to organise herself for their journey ahead.

Darcy smiled and nodded. 'I'd love to.'

'I don't think you'll find them as cool as unicorns though,' Felix teased, as Marta carried Luna over in her little gold cage and gently scooped her out onto Darcy's lap.

'Hi, Luna,' whispered Darcy, giving her a timid stroke. After a briefly suspicious sniff, Luna seemed to decide this was allowable and curled into a ball on Darcy's lap, falling back into a light doze. Marta took the opportunity to pluck a spine from Luna's back and tucked it away into her cloak pocket for later. As calm as ever, Luna barely stirred and Marta put her back into her cage to rest.

Bella also greeted her giant pet snail, Dorothy, giving her a large chunk of cucumber and slice of cuttlefish to enjoy. 'They're her favourite,' she explained to Darcy, lifting out a small, slime saturated log from Dorothy's enclosure and placing it into a glass jam jar. She twisted the lid tightly closed. 'If Neptune is right, this will give us a bright enough lamp to use in the mine if we need it.'

Eli and Felix were also readying themselves, loading satchels with things they might need for their journey. Eli packed his compass and trusty elvish map. While Felix stashed his new bejewelled lamp and plenty of snacks, even raiding his secret stash of lavender cookies. They each layered themselves with coloured jumpers and thick winter robes. The mine was very far away and while they didn't know exactly what to expect on their journey, they suspected it would be cold. Marta wrapped Darcy in a new, heavier deep pink cloak, and Darcy hoisted her wooden shield up onto her shoulder once again. They looked every bit the pack of intrepid explorers, ready for the adventure ahead.

Looking around at the tranquillity of their plush room, it was easy to feel like nothing had changed. But the friends knew differently. They knew they were about to embark on an adventure of a lifetime. One that would surely be dangerous, but also necessary. They would find a way to get Darcy home, and if they could, restore the magic of the realm. It was the right thing to do and they knew they had to try, whatever the cost.

'Are we all ready?' asked Marta, mothering the group as always with her tender and caring nature.

They gathered on the rug in the middle of the room, forming a close circle. From a little pink leather pouch in her pocket, Marta poured a small heap of shimmering fairy dust into each of their hands. It didn't feel as Darcy was expecting from the way it looked, like powder-soft sand from the Caribbean. It reminded her more of fine, but coarse sugar, slightly abrasive and rough to touch, but not uncomfortable. It shimmered the colour of perfectly cut diamonds.

Bella and Marta each took hold of Darcy's hands, keeping her safe in the middle of them. Before Darcy arrived in their realm, they would have never imagined it would be possible for a human to realm jump. But believing in the strength of the magical bond that Bella and Darcy shared, they trusted that this would be enough for them to realm jump together.

'Remember what Professor Fairweather said in our first lesson,' instructed Eli. 'All we have to do is picture exactly where we want to go. So, everyone imagine the mine in front of them.'

Following along intently, they closed their eyes, surrounding themselves with visions they had seen in the magical book. They tried to picture the dark grey, rocky exterior marking the entrance to the mine and the gaping mountainous mouth that would greet them.

'On the count of three, we throw the fairy dust up in front of us,' prompted Bella.

They all took a deep breath and counted in unison. 'One… two… three…', simultaneously launching their handfuls of fairy dust high up into the air in front of them. It hung there briefly, suspended in space and time as a sparkling cloud. Linking hands, they stepped through the blanket of glittering dust, travelling together into the unknown.

'I feel sick,' grumbled Darcy as she staggered to regain her balance after their realm jump. Luckily, Felix caught her just before she hit the floor. She bent forward, letting the blood rush back to her head and tried her best not to retch.

'Take a moment to catch your breath, Darcy,' he told her kindly. 'Realm jumping made some of us a bit woozy too the first time around, so I can't imagine it's very easy for humans.' He reached into Eli's rucksack and handed her a bottle of water to sip on, while the others gathered around Eli's magical map, trying to get their bearings.

The other side of the sparkling cloud of fairy dust revealed a sparse, unforgiving landscape. The ground stretched out in front of them like a bright, white, crystallised sheet, reflecting the sun in a way that seemed both dazzling and dangerous. It reminded Darcy of a large salt plain she had once seen on TV. A desolate space that seemed to sprawl on relentlessly for miles and miles in every direction.

While they were used to vast spaces throughout the fairy realm, these were usually filled with bright colours, tropical flowers and lush greenery. Here, however, nothing grew. The landscape instead remained bare, with the exception of a few small, twig-like shrubs. Mere skeletons of life and a nod to what this land could have been if it hadn't been decimated and neglected by goblins. It was a poignant reminder of just how destructive greed and selfishness could be. And it was growing worse each day with the ever-fading supply of magic throughout the realm.

Without shade, the sun beat down mercilessly on the friends. It was so much warmer here than they were expecting and they were now regretting the decision to wear thick, protective cloaks. They began removing some of their outer layers and stuffed them into their rucksacks, certain they would come in handy later.

Eli resumed examining his magical map, trying to figure out exactly where they had landed. He turned slowly, holding the map out in front of him and watching intently for any sign of life or a landmark to appear. Nothing. A bead of sweat trickled down his cheek, falling onto the magical map below. The map guzzled the droplet of liquid, greedily absorbing it into its fibres.

As if grateful for the hydration, slowly but surely, small, scattered scrawls started to appear on its surface. They were sparse, but they were visible. Eli was delighted as they appeared, assuring him that they had in fact made it to the outskirts of the mine.

'We're nearly there,' Eli sighed in relief. 'We just need to keep walking in that direction.' He pointed to a faintly visible set of grey rocks in the distance.

'Is that the mine?' asked Bella.

'It sure is,' Eli replied confidently. 'It shouldn't take much more than an hour or so to reach from here.'

'Well done, Eli,' Marta smiled proudly at her brother. 'We better get to it then.' They picked up their rucksacks and dusted themselves down.

As the friends trekked across the plain, they looked like conspicuous dots of colour smudged onto the white, vast background. If they had been spotted like this, they would surely be caught. They were increasingly grateful that no one else seemed to be around, as there were not many places to hide. Although, given the harshness of the landscape, this was perhaps not a surprise. Only fairies who didn't know what they were walking into would venture out in this.

Eventually, the pin pricks of grey in the distance started to grow closer, and after what felt like an eternity, it finally became clear that they were in fact not small rocks at all, but actually great, large charcoal boulders. Eli had been right. It was the entrance to the mine that they'd been looking for. As suggested by their magical book, these giant stones were stacked high and unevenly into a wonky archway that framed a dark, gaping cave. The cave seemed to at least provide some form of shade for the area, giving just enough shadow for small plants and fresh shoots to grow, framing the mine with the only greenery they had seen since they arrived. It was the only visible sign that the mine resembled anything magical and it made them feel instantly comforted.

With heavy legs, the friends shook off their rucksacks and sat down on the floor to rest. The ground was slightly moist and spongey, providing much relief after the hot walk they had just endured. Felix passed round their water bottles and even shared his prized lavender cookies.

'Great work, Eli,' praised Bella.

'Thanks,' he smiled back while stuffing himself with another lavender cookie. 'These really are delicious, Felix.'

'Yeah, Felix,' agreed Marta. 'Who'd have known you were such a star baker?'

Felix chuckled. 'I can't take all the credit. It's my mother's recipe actually. She always said the secret ingredient was a pinch of cinnamon, but I've never been sure. I've always thought it might be something more exotic, but she'll deny that if you ask her.'

The friends relaxed, enjoying a moment of tranquillity before they continued their quest. In the midst of their merriment, they remained blissfully unaware of the dangers that surrounded them. That is, until Darcy's gemstone necklace started to glow.

'Darcy, your necklace,' worried Bella.

It was only then they realised they had failed to notice the sound of heavy footsteps approaching. Darcy's gemstone continued to flicker, this time more urgently. Her magical wooden shield transformed spontaneously before her eyes into pure platinum.

'That must be what the scroll meant,' she exclaimed, feeling instantly relieved at the extra protection. The shield felt strong and reliable by her side.

'Quick, hide,' instructed Marta.

'Where?' whispered Eli, hoping not to draw further attention to them.

Bella scanned around quickly, pointing to a large rock behind them. 'Behind that boulder.'

But they were too late.

Chapter Nineteen

'Nice try,' bellowed a deep, rumbling voice belonging to a huge and hideous goblin. It stomped out aggressively from behind a nearby boulder, blocking their escape route. The friends weren't sure how something so large and loud could have snuck up on them so easily. Judging from its heavy thudding footsteps, miserable demeanour and raspy breathing, it must have just finished a shift mining for magic dust. It swaggered towards them with suddenly bright eyes, like it had just won an unexpected prize. They hoped there wouldn't be others close behind. The friends didn't know how they would escape one angry goblin, let alone a pack. They had come close enough to goblins at the wish wielding competition, and had no desire to meet one personally.

'Well, well, well…' The goblin sauntered towards the group, eyeing each of them suspiciously. 'What do we have here then?'

The ugly, green creature loomed over them, leaning in just close enough for them to smell its revolting breath, tainted with the smell of raw, rotten fish. Although no goblins would win a prize at a beauty pageant, this one was particularly awful. It was a fat goblin with spiky ears; bald except for a greasy patch of hair and small, bristly strands that poked out from pus-coloured warts across its pointy chin. Darcy thought it was the most revolting creature she had ever seen. It was like something from a nightmare. The putrid smell made her retch.

The goblin waggled a knobbly finger at the friends as it continued to speak, 'It looks like we have a group of young fairies, clearly up to no good.'

Bella cleared her throat. She had a skill of being charming when she wanted to be and hoped she could talk their way out of this worrying situation. 'Not at all, mighty goblin.' She continued sweetly, 'We just got a bit lost, but we'll be back on our way now.' She ushered her friends to pick up their belongings and make a swift exit.

'Not so fast there, little fairies.' The goblin shifted to block them again. 'You know it's not safe up here, don't you?' it taunted, clearly enjoying the opportunity to create a spectacle. 'Especially for a young group of fairies like yourselves, all alone, wandering helplessly through goblin territory.' The goblin paused, running a rough tongue over the edge of its cracked lips. It smiled sinisterly to reveal a set of sharp, plaque-ridden teeth that still contained bits of food from its last meal. The goblin took another step forward until it was towering over them once more. He tutted, spitting out a piece of pale pink flesh that had been stuck in his teeth. Darcy now hoped that it was in fact fish. If a goblin would eat a fairy, it would definitely eat a human. She didn't want to stick around to find out.

Although goblins and fairy folk were known to at best tolerate each other since the ancient war, it was now clearer than ever that the friends were not welcome here. There was a palpable tension, built on a bitter legacy of rivalry that stretched back an eternity to when goblins were first banished and outcast to the far edges of the realm. Of course, the young fairies had always been told not to trust goblins. They had all heard the tales of malicious goblins and mysterious fairy disappearances, but had at least in part assumed these were all just stories, designed to scare young fairies into being good and staying close to home. However, the playful cruelty in this goblin's eyes now told a different story. One that could put them in real danger if they didn't make their escape soon.

The goblin bent down towards Felix, grabbing him by his dark green collar and lifting him by the scruff of his neck, just high enough that the tips of his toes could no longer touch the ground. Felix felt a sudden jolt of adrenalin pulse through him. He was a broad and athletic fairy, known for being brave and not easily intimidated. He had also grown up the youngest of six siblings, so knew how to stand his ground in a fight. He stared back at the goblin with quiet determination. This goblin had picked the wrong fairies to mess with and he was not going to be bullied by the great lump in front of him.

'You don't scare me,' Felix confronted the goblin rebelliously.

The goblin paused, clearly not expecting such a brazen response from a young fairy. After a moment's hesitation, the goblin broke into a gravelly chuckle. It started small, but eventually built into an unexpected crescendo – a deep, villainous belly-laugh that caused the goblin to loosen its grip on Felix, who slipped out of its rough grasp and landed back on the ground below with a thump.

'I should scare you,' the goblin said menacingly as it swiped the last few tears of malicious laughter from its eyes. 'But luckily I've already eaten today, so I'm not in the mood for any more fairy flesh.'

Although the friends couldn't be sure if the goblin was telling the truth, or just trying to scare them, something about its expression told them it meant it. This warning was enough to know they were walking a dangerous path by provoking it further. They cowered into a group waiting to see what the goblin would do next. Eli searched for a way out, discreetly looking the goblin up and down for any source of inspiration.

While goblins were certainly not known for their sense of humour, they were also not known for their fashion sense. The goblin wore a dirty beige tunic, stained with patches of charcoal-blue dust from where it had been working in the nearby mine. It also carried a crystal pickaxe that it now waved at them threateningly, in between using it to pick out further chunks of putrid flesh from its gruesome mouth. Eli suspected the axe was made of diamond, the only substance tough enough to mine fairy dust. He also noticed the gold hilt was adorned with large rubies and sapphires. An unusually opulent choice for the average miner goblin. As goblins rarely took the time to nurture the earth around them, they faced the choice of either living frugally, or stealing and trading to fund a more lavish lifestyle. Based on the gemstone-studded axe it carried, Eli suspected this goblin may fall into the latter category, which could perhaps mean their safety could also be bought. They might be in luck.

'But there may still be something you can do for me, so I can let you go with a clear conscience, you see,' the goblin continued appraising them. It searched them up and down, looking for anything valuable enough to seize. The goblin's gaze landed firmly on Darcy and her glowing necklace, making Bella and Marta shift uncomfortably next to her. 'That's a very pretty necklace you have there, my dear.' The goblin eyed her suspiciously. 'It almost looks like a jewel from the mine.'

Thinking quickly on his feet, Eli grabbed the jewelled lamp that was stowed in Felix's rucksack, waving it at the goblin to draw its attention. Fortunately, the distraction worked. The goblin's head snapped round, mesmerised by the glistening gold and shimmering gems that now shone in its face.

'Well, I never…' the goblin stuttered, dumbfounded. 'Could it possibly be… is that a genie lamp?'

'You and I both know there's only one way to find out,' Eli responded coolly. 'You have to rub it to see if a genie appears.'

The goblin stared at the lamp eagerly with desperate, wide eyes. 'Can I touch it?' it asked, almost a grovel.

Eli paused a moment, pretending to consider the goblin's question. 'It's all yours if you let us go,' he replied, hoping to barter for their escape.

It was then the goblin's turn to ponder. Momentarily freed from the spell of the lamp, it gazed back and forth between its captives and its prize, trying to decide which it wanted more.

'You better make your mind up fast,' pressured Eli, 'or I'm sure another goblin will be out here soon who will be more open to a trade.'

The goblin could wait no longer. Overcome by a combination of greed, shimmering jewels, and the prospect of a genie who could grant its every desire, it yearned for the lamp. 'Very well,' it conceded.

'And one more thing…' Eli added boldly as a final point of negotiation. 'How do we get into the mine unseen?'

Lusting after the golden, wish-filled lamp, the goblin replied begrudgingly, 'Wait until dusk when the goblins will be leaving and sneak in through the emergency shaft round the back of the cave.'

'Thank you,' smiled Eli, 'that wasn't too difficult now, was it?'

He tossed the lamp towards the goblin's giant hairy feet, forcing it to dive forwards to save its new treasure. The goblin cradled the precious lamp and fortunately stuck to its word, leaving the friends behind, alone once more. They quickly scurried behind a tall pile of nearby rocks, hiding out of sight until nightfall.

'Phew,' breathed Darcy.

'That was amazing, Eli,' whispered Bella.

Felix agreed. 'Incredible, mate.'

'I am so proud of you, you giant smarty pants,' praised Marta, wrapping him up in a tight hug.

'Thanks all,' Eli exhaled for what felt like the first time all day. 'I could definitely do with another lavender cookie right about now,' he laughed. 'Who else is hungry?'

The friends rested and snacked secretively on more cookies until the sun started to sink below the horizon. They'd come too far to back out now and they were ready to make their move.

Chapter Twenty

As dusk turned to nightfall, the sky's purple hue became a deep inky blue, dotted with serene stars. It was a clear night on the edge of the realm. Without much cover from clouds, the friends felt surprisingly cold. They wrapped themselves back up in their thick winter cloaks, grateful they had brought them along to begin with. They sat quietly behind a group of large boulders, waiting patiently as the last group of goblins gathered up their gear to leave the mine. They looked just as grotesque as the last goblin they had encountered and stomped out just as aggressively. They chatted boisterously, packing away their axes and overalls, while boasting about who had mined the most fairy dust and earned the most gold coins from the royal treasury. The friends stayed quiet, careful not to make a sound and remaining hidden out of sight until the raucous goblin shrieks faded so far into the distance that they could no longer be heard. If they could help it, they did not want to face another goblin as long as they lived.

Once the friends were sure the coast was clear, they crept out from their hiding place behind the rocks and began cautiously making their way to the back of the mine.

'The entrance must be around here somewhere,' whispered Eli, scanning over the rough, rocky exterior for any sign of a door. They weren't quite sure what to look for, but they suspected it would be fairly obvious. After all, goblins weren't exactly known for their intelligence.

As if on cue, Felix spotted a round rusty metal handle that looked like it had been welded into the surrounding stone. 'Over here, everyone,' he called his friends closer, 'I think this might be the door. Although it doesn't look like it's been used in some time.'

Felix gave the handle a gentle tug to begin with, testing its strength. At first it failed to budge, but with more pressure, the hinges finally began to comply. Although it took most of Felix's strength, with a stubborn groan, the heavily disguised stone door creaked ajar.

Before Felix could peek into the darkness behind, Bella tugged him back, pulling her friends into a brief huddle. It reminded Darcy of watching her favourite football matches, where the team would gather before kick-off to talk tactics.

'We don't know exactly what we're going to face in there, so before we go in, I firstly just want to say, I love you all.' She smiled round at each of her friends in the circle and continued, 'But more importantly, stay vigilant at all times and if there's any sign of trouble, we get out, okay?'

They all nodded in agreement.

'Hopefully Darcy's necklace will warn us of any problems,' added Eli.

'And we also have an extra trick up our sleeve,' said Marta, pulling Luna's invisibility spine out of her cloak pocket. 'Literally,' she added. She removed her glove and held the spine up in front of her in her bare hand, suddenly making it disappear into thin air.

'That's amazing,' exclaimed Darcy, unable to keep herself from spontaneously giggling.

'That's nothing,' giggled back Marta's voice, seemingly from nowhere. 'If you all link hands with me and form a chain, we'll all become invisible together and can sneak in easily,' she advised. 'Neptune assures me that as long as I'm holding onto Luna's spine, we'll stay hidden from anyone around.'

'But it will only make us invisible, not inaudible,' prompted Eli, 'so we'll have to remember to stay quiet.'

The friends did as instructed: linking hands with Marta, Darcy and Bella at the front, followed by Felix and Eli. They took a deep breath and stepped through the hidden door, pulling it closed behind them so it didn't look suspicious.

At first, the mine seemed nothing more than a blur of blackness. Devoid of light, it temporarily consumed them like a black hole. After a few blinks, their eyes began to adjust to the new world around them, slowly noticing shimmers of grey-blue and turquoise fairy dust that glittered, muted from within the surrounding walls. Darcy imagined this must be what it felt like travelling into space. An eerily quiet and dark environment, undeniably dangerous, but with an almost indescribable beauty. The walls of the cave even shimmered cosmically, as if they were painted with stardust.

Moving as one, the friends carefully followed the path in front of them. It was narrow and seemed to spiral round and round, like a coiling snake. They walked cautiously, taking their time to leave nothing more than small footprints behind, which sat crisply in the fine layer of glitter that covered the floor. It was like walking through the first snow of winter. Magical, but fleeting.

When they finally felt like they had reached the centre of the mine, the narrow path changed abruptly, opening into a gigantic cavern that stretched high above them. The dark ceiling shimmered with so much fairy dust that it looked like the night sky. Eli wondered if he'd got so dizzy on their walk that they had actually found themselves back outside again under the canopy of stars.

As they walked further into the cavern to explore, they noticed the centre was occupied by a large and mysterious hole, blocked off with thick silver rope. They stepped closer to the edge of the strange hole to inspect it. Darcy shuddered at what she saw – a steep drop that seemed to fall downwards as far as the eye could see. It felt like the inside of a massive sinkhole, succumbing to the earth below. For as long as she could remember, she had always been afraid of heights. While she had never experienced any particularly traumatic falls while growing up, she found the idea of free-falling into the unknown utterly terrifying. Picking up on Darcy's sudden nervousness, Bella squeezed her hand in silent reassurance.

As far as the friends could make out, the giant hole was framed by a thin spiral staircase that had been carved into the surrounding rock. Although it was narrow, it looked sturdy. They assumed it must be the main entrance the goblins used to get down into the mine. Knowing how heavy a goblin could be, they felt certain the staircase would easily support them all. They paused briefly at the top of the stairs, before carefully starting their descent, step by step, down the stone staircase.

The staircase had a thin rope banister, but not much else for support. Not that it was very helpful to the friends while they linked hands, concealed by the invisibility spine that Marta held at the front. They took their time, steadily descending, guided by firefly lamps that were welded to the surrounding walls at regular intervals. The lamps cast a gentle orange glow against the charcoal stone, making the fairy dust within shimmer like tiny emeralds. It gave them just enough light to see.

After several loops of the gigantic spiral staircase, the steps mercifully straightened and levelled out to flat ground. Here, the familiar cinnamon-rich scent of fairy dust hung strongly in the air, stinging their nostrils. Eli guessed this must be the first mining level. Marta clutched the invisibility spine tighter. They didn't know if anyone else was around and they hoped very much not to find out.

They moved together quietly along the passage, following the strong smell of magic. Bella knew they must be approaching the open mine as there was a luminous turquoise glow slowly growing around them, as if inviting them in. The colour reminded Darcy of her own gemstone necklace.

As the friends turned a corner, Marta stopped suddenly, halting the group in a stack behind her. She pointed over to a charcoal wall in front where the bright blue light was coming from. It had been cracked open viciously with hammers and pickaxes, revealing glittering shards of sapphire magic, ready to be mined and ground. Indeed, below it sat three hessian sacks, already half full of the glittering dust. The goblins had been busy.

At the back of the group, Felix used his free hand to wave down his friends' attention. He pointed urgently towards the other side of the cracked stone wall. There, high on the wall, was a large ebony hawk, sat proudly with sharp yellow talons that tightly gripped its golden perch. The hawk wore a small white leather cap, with an unmistakable golden crest. It was the royal watch hawk.

The queen was well known for her love of animals, and had a particular fascination with ornithology. She had a vast collection of tropical and exotic birds, but her favourite by far was her noble watch hawk, Artemis. The queen hand reared Artemis from a hatchling and she had since become a trusted confidante. Nowadays, Artemis had great royal responsibilities for overseeing and reporting back to the queen on her most important projects. Smart, shrewd and with powerfully sharp predatory senses, it made sense that the queen had asked Artemis to guard the mine on her behalf.

Fortunately in that moment, Artemis napped on her perch, unaware of the invisible friends below. The friends crept forwards, trying to pass by silently. However, the strong smell of cinnamon was overwhelming. The heavy scent infiltrated Darcy's nostrils and filled her lungs, making them feel like they were on fire. Despite trying to stifle the feeling, her lungs betrayed her. She could no longer contain herself and burst into a spluttering fit of loud coughs. The sound made Marta jump, dropping the invisibility spine onto the dusty floor and revealing the friends to the world once again.

Artemis' bright yellow eyes shot open in response. Her blood-red pupils narrowed in on the now visible group beneath her. Without hesitation, she let out a spine-chilling shriek, squawking in alarm until the sound of heavy footsteps and clanking metal could be heard running from the distance.

A trio of armed guards charged towards them with full silver breastplates and long metallic spears, decorated with the same crest as Artemis' cap. Shocked by what they saw, the royal guards cornered the friends, trapping them in place.

'What do we do with them now?' asked one confused-looking guard to the others.

'The queen will want to hear about this,' another responded. 'She will decide what to do with them.'

Artemis squawked in agreement.

'Very well then,' supported the third guard. 'Let's take them back to the castle.'

With seemingly little effort, the strong guards scooped up the friends one by one, locking them in a rusty steel cage and dumping it on the back of a rickety mining cart to be driven back to the castle. Artemis perched herself possessively on top, watching them all with silent scrutiny. The friends could do nothing except huddle together, fearful of what might come next.

Chapter Twenty-One

The journey up to the castle was long and bumpy. With frequent sharp bends and rocky pathways, the friends had grown accustomed to being thrown around their rusty cage. They huddled together, bracing themselves for the next turn where they would no doubt be slammed into the metal walls of their cage once again. Bella silently wondered if the cart driver was doing it on purpose, or if he was purely incompetent. Based on his overly cheerful humming, she suspected the former. She rolled her eyes. His lack of tunefulness was already punishment enough.

Despite this, the journey was also proving uncomfortable for other reasons. As the cart rattled up another steep cobbled street, the friends grew increasingly nervous of what was to come. Their apprehension was only heightened by the way Artemis watched them, making them feel like criminals. Artemis eyed Darcy and her gemstone with particular suspicion, as if she already knew she was human. As much as they hated to think about it, they knew it was only a matter of time until their secret was revealed. They hoped her disguise was good enough to hold out.

Up ahead, the dramatic outline of the royal castle finally came into view. Its sharp edges scratched the skyline, imposing its presence over the realm below. Striking as it was, Darcy thought it looked like something from a fairy tale. With multiple sweeping balconies dipped in gold, and tall, cream turrets with sugared-lilac caps, she imagined it would be the perfect place for a princess to live. Indeed, on any other occasion, the friends would all agree that the castle looked magnificent. But given the present circumstances, even Marta couldn't seem to summon any enthusiasm for it.

Their wagon climbed the winding gravel driveway that was lined with citrus trees. The scent reminded Darcy of the smell of freshly squeezed lemonade on a hot summer day. It was something she would usually love, filled with memories of her childhood, but today it seemed overwhelming and bitter.

With a final creak up the gravel path, the cart finally came to a stop on the cobbled drive outside the main entrance to the castle. Their arrival had been expected and several armed guards dressed in the same uniform as those from the mine rushed over to meet them, wasting no time in hoisting the captives from their cage. The guards carried them roughly through the rose-gold portcullis, quickly bypassing the opulent lobby and descending into a dank dungeon below the castle floor. One by one, the friends were thrown into their shared prison. It was a small and dark space, kept cold by the surrounding stone. Eli was pleased he couldn't see much. Between the stale air and rancid smell, he didn't want to know what else was around them. With a final victorious squawk from Artemis at the top of the stairs, the heavy steel trapdoor was slammed shut with a loud echo. The friends were alone once more. Cold. Scared. And at the mercy of their captors.

'Is everyone okay?' Bella whispered into the darkness.

'Yes,' whispered back Eli and Felix.

'Just about,' agreed Marta. 'How about you, Darcy?'

'I'm okay. Better here than with the goblins,' she replied. 'Although I think we could do with an escape plan about now,' she added with mild sarcasm, trying to disguise her nervousness.

Bella laughed quietly beside her. 'Well, at least your sense of humour is still intact.'

'You're right though, Darcy,' added Felix. 'We could do with getting out of here. ASAP! Who knows what trouble we'll get into if we stay here much longer? And I don't even want to think about what they'll do to us if they find out Darcy is human.'

Eli pondered. 'Do you still have some fairy dust, sis?' he asked Marta. 'Perhaps we could use that to realm jump again?'

'Great idea, Eli,' responded Marta. 'I think a lot spilled out of my pocket on the journey, but I might still have enough left.' She began rummaging through her pocket to see what she could salvage. It didn't feel like much, but they knew a little magic could go a long way if they all believed in it.

While Marta tried to gather as much fairy dust as possible, the friends heard the trapdoor above swing open. They froze in place, unsure what would happen next. Within moments, two well-dressed maids entered the dungeon, silently lighting a series of small, lilac candles and placing these on wooden ledges around the room. They smelt like calming lavender and cast a soft yellow glow that bathed the small space in just enough light that the friends could now see each other. It also provided some much-needed and reassuring warmth. When the maids had finished, they left back up the stairs as silently as they had entered.

The next unexpected sound was that of gentle footsteps steadily descending the stairs. The friends glanced at each other uneasily, unsure of who would be visiting next, and with what motive. They hoped it wouldn't be another ruthless guard. Or Artemis. Or even worse, Principal Featherstone. When they did see the unexpected visitor appear in front of them, it left them both spluttering and speechless.

The queen entered the dungeon alone with an air of calm authority. As always, she was dressed elegantly, but today she had opted for a less formal look. Her long lilac skirt was paired with a cream blouse and large pearl jewellery that emphasised her silver bun and blonde highlights. She looked regal, but also more approachable than they had ever seen her before at meetings and events. She also looked tired, with small bags forming under her darkened eyes.

Unsure how to react and still in awe of the queen's presence, Marta quickly stood up. She wasn't sure of correct royal protocol, but had always wanted to meet the queen and make a good impression, even in these circumstances. She offered up a slightly awkward half-curtsy as a sign of respect and sat back down. A small grateful smile played at the edge of the queen's mouth, but she remained composed. It was clear something was bothering her and she was eager to make this interaction quick. She began her questioning.

'My faithful Artemis tells me you have all been snooping around the ancient magic mine,' she stated bluntly. 'As you well know, this is a very dangerous place for young fairies to be, so I am quite sure you must have a very good reason for being out there by yourselves. Would you care to enlighten me?' she asked shrewdly, glancing at each of them in turn to decide which of the friends would be first to crack. Her eyes landed back on the pretty blonde half-elf dressed in deep pink.

Feeling pressured to respond, Marta babbled, 'This has all been one giant misunderstanding, Your Majesty. We'd quite like to go back to the academy now, please, if that's okay?' Her friends nodded in agreement, hoping they could once again talk themselves out of trouble.

The queen knew she was onto something and continued pressing. 'Well, I'm sure that can be arranged, but first, I really must get to the bottom of this. It is highly irregular behaviour and I expect more from my subjects,' she added sternly. 'Perhaps I should call Principal Featherstone to deal with you?' she threatened. 'I am sure she would be most alarmed to hear what her students have been up to without her knowledge.'

The friends fidgeted in clear discomfort at the thought of their principal hearing about their escapades. The last thing any of them wanted was to be expelled, but at this rate, it wasn't looking good. They were worried they'd even be convicted of treason and banished forever.

'Please don't call Principal Featherstone,' grovelled Eli timidly, about to give in and spill their plans.

'Stop,' demanded Bella boldly, unable to hear her friends squirm any longer. 'I'll tell you everything, if you let my friends go.'

It was now the queen's turn to be shocked. She had never been spoken to with such audacity, but she did appreciate the young fairy's loyalty and determination. The fairy reminded her somewhat of a younger, more spirited version of herself.

'Very well,' the queen agreed, slightly bemused.

Bella took a deep breath. 'We know the toadstool is running out of magic.' She was unsure how the queen would respond, and for a moment it looked like she would deny it. Bella persevered, 'Please don't lie to us, Your Highness, we overheard everything at a secret meeting of the Fairy Council in our enchanted library.'

Unexpectedly, the queen sighed and sank down onto the floor next to the friends in defeat. There was no point in trying to cover it up now. She was worried the news would soon be out across the whole realm anyway. 'Alas, it is true,' she confirmed mournfully. 'That is why Artemis and my guards were at the mine. We have been trying to dig for more magic dust until we can find a proper cure.'

Although it came as no surprise to the friends, it was remarkably sad to hear the truth in person. The situation seemed grave to begin with, let alone the fact that those in charge didn't know how to fix it. They slumped down in glum reflection until something suddenly caught the queen's eye – a shimmer of blue she had previously failed to recognise. Deep in thought, she turned to look at Darcy's iridescent gemstone, then stared intensely into Darcy's hazel eyes. Although not uncomfortable, it felt strange to Darcy, a bit like when a stranger stares too long, trying to recall where they've seen you before.

The queen's voice softened. 'What is your name?'

'Darcy Holloway,' she replied truthfully, despite feeling suddenly unsure of herself.

'And you are human?' the queen asked, giving the distinct impression that she already knew the answer. Darcy nodded, hoping that her response would not land them in any more trouble.

The queen smiled back gently. 'Perhaps it is fate then that you are all here.' Noticing the puzzled expressions on each of the friends' faces, the queen continued, 'I recognised that necklace as soon as I saw it. I should have spotted it sooner.' She shook her head. 'It is one of our precious gemstones – one of the original five from the ancient mine, each as old as our realm itself and each with a unique gift.'

'The ones from the stories?' asked Eli inquisitively, hoping to confirm what he already believed.

The queen nodded and turned to look directly at Darcy once again. 'You may have already realised that yours contains a protective charm. It has been passed down through generations of your family and acts as a magical key that connects you to our world. The fact that you are here, right now, in our time of need, gives me great hope. We may yet be able to restore the magic of our land and there might be something you can do to help.'

Blown away by what she had heard, Darcy remained speechless. Although shocked to her core, she had always believed in fairies and magic, and in her heart she believed what the queen had said to be true. The gemstone must be why she had felt so comfortable since being here and more connected than ever to her mother. Sensing Darcy's wave of emotion, Bella reached out and squeezed her hand in reassurance.

'I think it's time you learn the truth about everything,' the queen added. 'If you're ready to hear it, I'd like to take you to my royal library.'

Chapter Twenty-Two

The royal library was as opulent as they had expected, but also unusual. Set inside a large rectangular glass bubble, it felt more like a greenhouse than a library. This feeling was enhanced by the large variety of tropical plants and flowers that climbed each wall, creating a jungle-like oasis in the middle of the castle grounds. In the centre of the room was a short, flamingo-shaped fountain that bubbled gently into a small pool below. The pool whirled into a narrow, gargling stream that meandered its way through the library, winding around the room to create several secluded nooks and crannies, each framed with meticulously carved ornate bookshelves and decorated with plush sofas and scatter cushions. The perfect place to sit and read quietly or steal some time alone.

'I've always loved this room,' the queen sighed, recalling the awe she felt when she first entered the library. 'In fact, it might be one of my favourites in the whole palace.' She explained to her guests, 'My late father designed it as a gift for my mother, who always loved to read and being close to nature. Unfortunately, with the responsibilities of running a realm, they were unable to travel as much, so he wanted to create her own personal paradise, where she could slip away to explore new places and dream up visions of new adventures. It became even more of a gift when she fell ill.'

'It's breathtaking,' beamed Darcy.

'Incredible,' agreed Marta.

'Thank you,' smiled the queen. 'Please help yourself to refreshments and take a seat,' she instructed, gesturing to a grand sofa by the fountain. To its side was a marble table, almost overflowing with delicate floral tea sets, jugs of fresh lemonade and a fine spread of scones, cream, jams and marmalade. It was a feast that Felix in particular didn't need to be invited twice to indulge in. He piled a china plate high with scones and lashings of jam and cream and sat down next to his friends on the sofa with a ginormous grin plastered across his face.

When everyone was comfortable, the queen began. 'I am sure you are all familiar with our sad tales of the Great Goblin War?' The friends nodded. 'While it was true that the goblins wanted control of our realm, they also wanted more. What they truly sought was untapped power and magic of their own. To get this, they attempted to collect the five precious gemstones that originally came from the ancient magic mine. Ones such as the pendant that Darcy is wearing now.' She gestured to Darcy with a smile. 'Legend has it that when combined, these gemstones will form The Celestial Wand, the most powerful magical object known to our realm. This wand is rumoured to contain unlimited power which, depending on the users intent, could either be used to restore peace, balance and magic to the land, or cause mass destruction and devastation,' she added with a sombre expression. 'The catch is that not only must you collect all five gemstones, but in order to wield their power, they must be combined by a worthy human and a fairy godmother that share an unbreakable bond.' The queen paused for breath, taking a sip of cherry blossom tea. 'The goblins thought they had found this with their white-cloaked fairy godmother, their leader, but they only had possession of one gem, the Protection Stone that Darcy now carries. They pillaged and raided our lands to try to find the others, but were fortunately unsuccessful.'

'But, Your Majesty,' began Eli curiously. 'Where were the gemstones? And what happened to them after we defeated the goblins?'

'Well,' the queen replied, 'after the war, we believed the Protection Stone was lost to time.' She paused and chuckled, glancing over at Darcy. 'Although I can now see that it's been put to good use in the human realm. Thankfully, however, we still had possession of the four other gemstones and had created the Fairy Council to protect the realm. We decided it would be prudent to delegate the responsibility of caring for each stone to a different Council member, entrusting each owner to hide and protect their gem, without anyone else knowing where it was kept. We felt this would be the safest option to prevent their power from falling into the wrong hands and causing another war.'

The friends looked round at each other, shocked and surprised to learn the truth about the war, the Fairy Council and Darcy's magical gemstone. Felix had barely even touched the scones and had since lost his appetite.

'I appreciate that's a lot to take in,' acknowledged the queen.

'It is, Your Majesty, but where do we all come in?' Bella asked, getting straight to the point in her typical robust fashion.

'I think you and Darcy share a deeply strong bond, Bella. After all, that connection is what has allowed you, a first-year fairy-godmother student, to bring a human into our realm through a rogue dream cast. That, and the connection Darcy shares to this realm through the Protection Stone,' explained the queen. 'Through your connection, I believe you both share the power needed to combine the gemstones and create the Celestial Wand. It won't be easy, but it will restore magic across our land and benefit both of our worlds greatly if you are able to achieve it.'

The queen continued, 'If you are willing to help save our realm, the first thing we must do is gather the stones; but before you choose, there is more you should know about them.' She began scanning a nearby bookshelf as if looking for something incredibly specific. After a few moments, her gaze landed on a large, white, leather-bound book. She lifted it down carefully from the shelf for everyone to see. Its thick grained cover was painted with five delicate gold symbols, one of which the friends already recognised. A small circle framed by two swans meeting by their beaks and tails.

'That is the symbol for your Protection Stone, Darcy,' explained the queen, following Darcy's gaze. 'The other symbols represent each of the other gemstones, and the bright white cover represents the pure power they combine to create – the Celestial Wand.' She opened the cover to reveal a floating hologram mirroring the iridescent purple-blue gem that hung around Darcy's neck.

'The thing you must understand about these magical gemstones is that each one contains great power, but this always comes at a price. This means that each gem is blessed with a gift, but also an unavoidable curse, which with time can become a great burden on the owner.'

The queen continued, 'Darcy's gemstone, for example, was given as a gift by the original white-cloaked fairy godmother to her human, an ancestor of the Holloway family. This is how I now believe it came to be in the human realm, Darcy, passed down through generations of your family tree.'

The friends nodded along, understanding so far.

'The fairy godmother hoped the gemstone would protect her human connection, keeping her as close to immortality as humanly possible. But that was not to be. Although the human was protected physically, they eventually passed away from a broken heart, leaving the white-cloaked godmother devastated. Over time the godmother became bitter and wicked through grief, turning into a power-hungry ally to the goblins and starting the war,' explained the queen.

'As I'm sure you know, the stone flashes as a warning whenever the wearer might be in danger, but, as we have learnt from the tale of white-cloaked godmother, its curse means it can only protect the owner from physical harm, not emotional distress. This emotion can be amplified, making sorrow feel heavy, like a blanket of endless grief.'

Darcy nodded. This feeling seemed to resonate with her more than ever since the passing of her mother. She took comfort in finding out that her emotions could have in fact been amplified by the gemstone. Just like everything in this realm, bit by bit, everything seemed to be making more sense. Being here was helping her to heal.

Next, the queen pointed to a symbol that looked like two interlocking triangles, forming a star. On this page was a rough green-and-blue gem that she explained to be the Realm Jumping Stone. 'This stone is currently guarded by Morgan Ivory, Chief of the Tooth Fairies. It contains all the power needed to visit other realms without a portal, but although the wearer can control where they appear, they cannot control when, and we all know that time can be a cruel mistress.'

Turning the page again, they were presented with a vision of a brightly coloured orange-yellow gemstone that practically radiated off the page, next to a small gold symbol of the sun and moon. 'This is the Shapeshifting Stone,' explained the queen. 'It gives the owner the power to change form, at will, into anything they desire. No fairy dust required. However, each time it is used, it costs a memory that cannot be chosen. It is currently cared for by our Pixie Leader, Eden Briar.'

'And what's this one here?' asked Eli, pointing to a symbol that looked like an old and wise tree, sat next to an image of a glowing white-grey, almost luminous stone.

'That is the Peace Stone,' the queen answered. 'It is one of the most powerful gems, giving the owner the ability to hear thoughts and understand different languages. But the price to pay is also steep. Each time it is used, the owner slowly loses their hearing, until they can no longer hear voices or thoughts at all. It is guarded by your kin, Aelfric Albion, Elder of the Elves.'

'And the fifth stone, Your Majesty?' asked Bella.

Pointing to the next page, emblazoned with the symbol of a Celtic love knot, the queen explained soberly, 'This is the Heart Stone.' She reached under her blouse and pulled out a delicate gold chain, supporting a smooth pendant of marbled red-and-pink stone. 'The Heart Stone has the power to make others love you, but only superficially, perhaps a bit like royal subjects.' She looked slightly ashamed. 'But this love will only ever be shallow and it means I can never truly experience unconditional, reciprocated love. At least not like the way my beloved father loved my mother,' she added sadly, glancing round the beautiful library.

Darcy felt a great pang of sympathy for the queen. She understood exactly what it felt like to feel love that could never again be fulfilled. She probed gently, 'So, what do we need to do when we've collected the other stones, Your Highness? How do we create the Celestial Wand?'

'As I understand, the stones will need to be combined using the strength of your magical bond. It will require a journey and a sacrifice, that much I know, but the specifics belong to an old elvish prophecy that for safety, only Aelfric knows. I suggest you visit him last and he will tell you where to go next.'

The friends stared round at each other as if silently communicating, just like the Summersong twins. One by one, they each turned to the queen and smiled.

'Does that mean you are willing to help save our realm?' the queen asked hopefully.

They nodded in unison. 'Yes, Your Majesty.'

The queen exhaled sharply. 'I am so thankful to you all. If you are able to achieve this, the realm will forever be in your debt.' She turned next to Darcy. 'I am so sorry you have found yourself in the middle of our plight. The fact you are choosing to help us, unselfishly and with such kindness and grace, makes you incredibly special. Your mother would be very proud.'

Darcy wiped away at a small tear forming in the corner of her eye as the queen continued, 'Be aware that the time may come when you have to make a hard decision on this journey, but I know your friends here will do all they can to look after you.'

'You can say that again,' interjected Bella, 'I promise to protect you till the day I become stardust.'

'And so do we,' added Marta, Eli and Felix together.

'Thank you, everyone,' grinned Darcy, 'but in truth you have already saved me. After a long time, I finally believe in magic again. I feel it running through me and I feel it in our bond, Bella. I know we can do this. Together.'

'Together,' they all rallied.

'If you're ready, then I best give you this for safekeeping.' The queen removed her Heart Stone necklace and placed it over Bella's neck. 'I suggest you start with Morgan and the Realm Jumping Stone. The Tooth Fairy Castle is a bit of a journey from here, so take my giant buzzards to fly there and conserve your energy. I'll also send Artemis with you to keep watch.'

Hearing her name, Artemis swooped into the library, landing gracefully on top of the flamingo statue in the middle of the fountain. Accepting her new companions, Artemis gave a graceful bow.

'And stock up on anything you like before you go,' added the queen. 'Help yourselves to refreshments and refill your fairy dust from my own personal collection.'

She indicated to a gold pot of fairy dust that had since appeared, twinkling in the corner of the room.

Regaining his appetite, Felix quickly scoffed down his scones. With Eli's help, they filled their rucksacks with as much food as they could manage, while Marta and Bella stashed pouches of fairy dust wherever they could. Darcy sat quietly for a moment beside the queen, apprehensive yet excited for the adventure ahead.

Chapter Twenty-Three

Perched precariously on top of the queen's giant pet buzzards, the friends clung onto handfuls of their soft giant feathers, bracing themselves to be catapulted into the sky. Artemis squawked loudly several times, as if in conversation with the buzzards, giving them directions to the Tooth Fairy Castle. When she had finished, the buzzards launched upwards on her command, taking care not to lose their precious cargo in the process. They eventually settled into a diamond formation, led at the front by Artemis.

'This view is incredible,' shouted Felix over the sound of wind rushing past his face and through his hair. He pulled the hood of his dark green cloak up tightly over his head to provide some shelter as they continued gliding, further and further away from the queen's castle.

Darcy agreed with Felix. She adored the feeling of flying and the sense of freedom it gave her. It was so easy to be fully present and in the moment while soaring through the sky; so much so, that any problems or worries faded into insignificance. The experience was almost meditative. Although it had to be said that the buzzards were not as fun as Snowdrop and her unicorn friends, twisting and diving through the clouds. Perhaps the buzzards also felt the pressure and urgency of the friends' mission to retrieve the precious gemstones.

After some time of peaceful gliding over quiet forests and serene fields, the lush green landscape below gave way to the majestic crystal lake that dominated the centre of the realm. Just like a mirror, it reflected their shimmering formation as they soared across it. But the friends knew there was more to the lake than met the eye. Their reflections glided alongside shadows of fish and undoubtedly other mysterious creatures that lurked below its surface.

'Look over there, Darcy,' advised Bella, pointing to the left of the lake. 'That's our toadstool.'

She stared over at the sagging giant red and white-spotted toadstool sat alone within a small emerald meadow. It didn't seem as bright or plump as she'd imagined. In fact, she thought it seemed rather sad, if it was possible for toadstools to feel that way. Darcy assumed it must be a side-effect of losing its magic.

'It's fading fast,' shouted Marta, as if reading Darcy's mind. They continued onwards, skating ahead to the large hill in the distance that housed the three fairy schools, including their own Hummingbird Academy.

The closer they flew, the more nervous they felt. They knew by now their classmates would be wondering where they had gone. Perhaps snobby Scarlett would have even told Principal Featherstone. A thought that worried them greatly. They didn't want to be expelled, but they knew they must continue their mission. After all, if they didn't succeed, there might not even be a school to come back to.

Despite Darcy's understandable naivety of the fairy realm, it was instantly obvious to her where they were heading. As expected, they eventually touched down outside a large porcelain-white-coloured castle, coated in a rough texture that from a distance looked like small pieces of popcorn and shimmered like pearls. Darcy was so mesmerised by the exterior that she reached out to stroke its rough surface, quickly retracting her hand when on closer inspection, she realised it was actually coated in tiny teeth in all shades of white and beige. Felix chuckled softly at her, changing her shocked expression into a giggle too.

They carefully climbed off their buzzards and followed Artemis towards a poorly concealed side door at the base of one of the castle's several enamel turrets. Oddly, this door seemed to be made of titanium, or some other kind of strong silver metal that was unlike the other doors nearby. It looked thick too, almost like the entry to a bank vault. Darcy wondered what they would find inside. It would surely be something precious.

They slipped through the heavy door into a large concrete basement, separated into alcoves by tall pillars illuminated by strips of bright, white light. It felt colder and more clinical than Darcy had been expecting. Not entirely unlike a garage from the old heist movies she used to watch with her mother, where thieves would gather to plot or divide their loot. Except here there was no sign of gold, bank notes or coins. Not even a sign of old milk teeth as she had half been expecting. It was just an empty, mostly grey, concrete space, and by far the dullest room she had seen since she had fallen through her dream world into this realm.

A shadow darted across the far side of the vault. From the slim frame and flash of auburn hair, it was clear it was Morgan Ivory, Chief of the Tooth Fairies. She was dressed smartly in a shiny, silver dress and chunky black boots. As serious as ever, she marched towards the friends and Artemis with her trademark chain of pearl teeth bobbing along to the beat of her walk. Although she tried to remain poker-faced, something hid behind her bright green eyes that looked like hope.

She nodded at Artemis as she approached, before addressing her guests directly, 'Welcome, friends.' She glanced over to the young girl adorned with the turquoise Protection Stone. 'And welcome to you in particular, Darcy.'

'Thank you, Ms Ivory,' answered Darcy courteously.

'Please, call me Morgan,' she responded gracefully, 'welcome to our Eternal Archive and Mint.'

'What exactly does that mean?' asked Felix curiously. 'What is it you do here?'

Morgan chuckled. 'I appreciate for fairy godmothers like you, this place may look rather dull and strange. But for us tooth fairies, this is the life-blood of our operation. Down here in the Mint is where we create all the money that we place under children's pillows. We must make sure that we always have enough for any child expecting to lose a tooth, in any country of the world, so it is a full-time job.' She paused, strolling over to a nearby concrete column.

'But perhaps the most interesting part of our vault, is our Eternal Archive.' She pulled a concealed lever on the side of the nearby column. The ground seemed to shake and rumble underneath them, like giant gears were grinding below the floor's surface. With a loud hum, a large metal tube rose up slowly from the concrete floor next to Morgan, like something from a sci-fi movie. She reached for a metal handle on the giant cylinder, which sprung open a hidden hatch within. The friends peered inside, noticing hundreds of thousands, maybe even millions, of tiny, clear glass jars, each containing a single tooth.

Morgan removed a single jar, holding it in her hand, up to the bright, white light for her guests to see. 'Locked within each of these precious vaults is every tooth we've ever collected, each containing a story of its own. When we take a tooth from under a pillow, we carefully store it here in our magically controlled environment and meticulously document everything about the tooth and the individual it came from.' She continued her explanation, 'Within each tiny jar, alongside the tooth itself, we include a miniature scroll with all the information we have gathered. We guard this knowledge here, keeping it safe for fairy-kind in case it is needed to help a child as they grow.'

'That's incredible,' said Marta, nearly speechless. 'You must know everything about every human who has ever existed.'

'Mostly,' agreed Morgan. 'Teeth are each as unique as fingerprints. Although they can't tell us everything there is to know about a person, they can tell us a lot;

from a person's age and gender, even through to their health and personality traits. Which brings me onto the business at hand.' She continued, 'Forgive me Darcy, but before I hand over my precious Realm Jumping Stone, I must know you are who I have been led to believe. We have been waiting for a special descendant from your bloodline for a long time. You are one of only a few humans who know of our existence, let alone have a bond and belief strong enough to create the Celestial Wand, so I must know that you are who you say.'

'Of course,' replied Darcy earnestly. 'What would you like to know?'

Morgan unscrewed the metal lid from the tiny glass jar, emptying the contents into her hand. She spent a moment examining the tiny bloodied tooth. It had a jagged edge that looked like it had been ripped away cruelly from the surrounding gums. When content, she placed it back in the jar and unravelled the dainty scroll. As she read, her brow furrowed, making her look for the first time anywhere near her actual age. She rolled the scroll up again and tucked it gently back into the glass jar, alongside the small tooth.

'Tell me, Darcy, when did you lose your last milk tooth?' she asked.

'Three years ago,' replied Darcy.

'And it was a significant day for you, wasn't it?' Morgan asked softly.

'Yes, it was my birthday,' she responded, slightly more timidly than before.

'But that's not all, is it?' Morgan probed gently, trying her best to be sensitive about the answer she had just read in the miniature scroll.

'No,' Darcy shook her head sadly. 'That was also the day my mother passed away,' she added, taking a deep breath. 'My tooth fell out in the same car accident that took her life.'

Darcy's eyes glistened at recalling the painful memory, but she refrained from crying. She instead chose to focus on the strength and solidarity she had found through her magical bond with Bella and her fairy friends. Bella stepped sideways to put an arm round her protectively and gave her a squeeze, bringing her back to the present moment.

'I'm so sorry to have made you relive that painful memory, Darcy,' replied Morgan with genuine sympathy. 'When the queen told me you had arrived and the prophecy would be fulfilled, I had to be sure with my own eyes. Everything you have told me aligns with what I have read and witnessed in the archive of your tooth, and I am therefore convinced that you are who we have been waiting for, thank you.'

Darcy nodded thoughtfully in response. It was difficult to remember such painful memories, but she was determined to do what needed to be done.

'It is now my duty to give you the Realm Jumping Stone, so you can continue your quest,' stated Morgan. She lifted off her necklace of tiny pearl teeth, feeling each tooth between her fingers like a string of prayer beads. When she had finally found the tooth she was looking for, she squeezed it tightly in the palm of her hand, applying just enough force that the delicate chain snapped, sending a cascade of teeth scattering and shattering across the hard, grey floor. She looked up at the friends and unclasped her hand, revealing a small green-blue stone sat in the middle of her palm.

'The Realm Jumping Stone,' exhaled Felix, amazed. It was only then he realised he'd said it out loud and not just in his own head.

Morgan laughed. 'That's right. This stone contains the power to travel between realms, but remember, although you can control where you visit with just a thought, the stone dictates the time period, so use it wisely.' She continued, 'The burdens of these stones are great, as well as the price of losing them, so I advise you each to only carry one.'

Sensing Felix's fascination with this particular stone, Morgan reached out and handed it to him, transferring it carefully from her palm to his. He took it gently, hiding it in his cloak pocket. With the warnings they had all been given, he hoped never to need use it, but should the situation demand, he knew he would be ready.

Morgan left them with one final instruction. 'While you're close by, I suggest you visit Pixie Hollow next to find the Shapeshifting Stone that Eden guards. But be warned, pixies like to play tricks, so keep your wits about you; there may be a surprise or two in store.'

Chapter Twenty-Four

Their visit to the Tooth Fairy Castle had been surprisingly positive, and if the friends admitted to themselves, it had all seemed a bit too simple. As they readied to leave, they said warm goodbyes to Morgan and promised to visit again soon when everything was back to normal. She gave them each a hug in return, wishing them well for the journey ahead and even offering them a place to study if they really did get expelled from the Hummingbird Academy as a result of their adventure. Although Morgan stressed that she had known their principal for a long time, and while she was strict, she was also fair, so Morgan expected her to excuse their absence given the circumstances. The whole visit left the friends feeling strangely optimistic, but they did not wish to become complacent. Morgan's warning still rang vividly in their ears. Pixies were not malicious by nature, but they were known to be mischievous, and at times deceitful. They knew they must be cautious and they would surely need to be cunning to collect their next stone. Their next visit would not be as easy as visiting the reliably natured tooth fairies.

Flanked by Artemis, they left the pearly gates of the Tooth Fairy Castle behind and began a slow trudge down the steep hill, back towards its base.

'I can't believe I just met an actual tooth fairy,' squealed Darcy. The friends chuckled at her excitement.

'And not even just any old tooth fairy…' Bella encouraged. 'It was the chief tooth fairy herself.'

'Quite an impressive operation they have going on there, to be fair,' chipped in Felix.

'And Morgan was really nice too,' added Eli. 'Who'd have known? We always thought tooth fairies were a bit uptight.'

'That's a bit rich coming from you,' teased Marta, poking fun at her little brother.

He chuckled back, 'Fair point, sis. Either way, getting this next stone definitely won't be as easy.'

Artemis squawked in agreement, ruffling her feathers.

'Yeah, you're right, Eli,' replied Felix. 'Pixies are known to be crafty. It makes total sense that Eden has the Shapeshifting Stone.'

'We'll have to keep our wits about us for sure,' chimed in Bella.

They continued down towards the tall purple hawthorn tree at the base of the hill. Known for wild parties and daily doses of pranks and general mischief, they would typically expect to hear the merriment at

Pixie Hollow before their saw it. However, the friends couldn't help but notice something strange as they approached the entrance. Where there would usually be small gangs of pixies whizzing around the old tree, or creating traps on the grass outside for unsuspecting visitors, there was no one to be found. Everything was suspiciously quiet, with only the blossoming branches of the giant purple tree stretched out to greet them.

'This is a bit odd, isn't it?' Bella whispered to Marta.

'Very,' she agreed.

They proceeded cautiously over to the base of the tree, keeping a close eye for any booby traps that might have been set along the way. Fortunately, on this occasion, their path seemed to be clear, allowing them to stroll up freely to the door that had been carved into the bottom of the tree, marking the entrance to the hollow. Expecting to meet some resistance from the wooden door, Bella gave it a strong tug. Surprisingly, it swung open, revealing an equally abandoned interior.

The friends stepped through into the hollow, which suddenly expanded in front of them into a large and unexpected sight – a grand theatre lobby, painted in antique cream and decorated at every opportunity in patterns of lavish gold leaf. In typical pixie fashion, it was clear that the outside of the hollow had been a trick in itself, concealing their true home within.

To the friends' left was a snack bar, piled high with little red-and-white popcorn cups, along with a sign that read 'Today's Show'. Underneath was a small chalkboard confirming why the hollow was so quiet: 'No Show Today – Toadstool Duty'.

'That must be where everyone is,' advised Marta. 'Things must really be getting bad if everyone is now taking shifts to care for the toadstool.'

The friends looked at each other solemnly. 'We better get on and find that stone then,' suggested Darcy.

They continued walking in the only direction they could, funnelled towards two red, draped curtains hanging at the back of the room. As they stepped through, they were met by an even grander sight. A huge theatre, framed by several rows of red velvet chairs which led down to a large stage front and centre. This was adorned by a sweeping golden arch and decorated with obnoxiously large golden masks depicting the Muses of comedy and tragedy. With the exception of the gaudy decoration, Darcy didn't think the grand theatre would look out of place in the West End.

The friends stared round dumbfounded. Artemis was the only one who seemed unsurprised. Sensing the friends trepidation, she took the lead, waving her wing to signal them to follow. They did as instructed, following her down the central aisle, up onto the stage and through the wings to the private backstage area.

As they passed through another set of velvet curtains, the room split off into several corridors. Each was lined with multiple doors marked with a gold star inscribed with the name of the pixie who lived there. The doors were decorated in different colours and with a variety of materials, allowing each pixie to show off their personality. Some were covered in glitter and sequins, some were scrawled in poetry, and others were painted with dramatic depictions of their favourite theatre scenes. The space was also messy, lined with racks upon racks of outfits and props. It made Darcy think of a fancy dress shop.

Following Artemis' lead, they eventually arrived at the final door in the corridor. Bigger than all the others, outlined in gold, and with the largest star in the centre, the decor said it all. They had reached their destination, the changing room of Eden Briar, Leader of the Pixies. Bella knocked twice to be polite, but received no answer. Undeterred, she twisted the golden handle and opened the door.

In keeping with her role as a Council member, and also her passion for the arts, Eden's room was part office and part dressing room. Although judging by the size of each of these areas, it was clear which role she preferred. On one side of the room was a modest-sized wooden desk, squeezed in next to a bric-a-brac bookshelf. This was all but eclipsed by an expansive white dressing table and huge mirror rimmed with bubble lights that took up the full width of the wall. The dresser was disorganised too, just like her scattered personality. Littered with multi-coloured jars and pots, undoubtedly full of lotions and potions used to create her theatrical looks.

'What is it with fairies and their fascination with glass jars?' Darcy puzzled out loud, ever so slightly bemused.

From a retro pink chair on the far side of the room, Eden Briar spun round slowly to greet her visitors. 'I've always wondered the same as it happens,' she greeted them playfully. 'You must be Darcy,' she added, staring at the human girl in front of her with fascination, 'I've been expecting you.'

Eden stood up in her long pink-and-green robe to examine her new guests and shake Darcy's hand. 'Sorry, we haven't been able to give you a proper welcome today,' explained Eden. 'We would usually relish the chance to perform for outside guests, but today it was our turn to monitor our precious toadstool. As you know, the situation is getting worse each day and we must now provide constant care, which is why only I stayed to meet you.'

'We're pleased you didn't go to too much trouble for us,' replied Darcy. 'We've just come to collect the Shapeshifting Stone.'

'Indeed, I am aware,' Eden agreed. 'But you must have heard that us pixies are known for making mischief and I am afraid this is no exception.' Throwing her head back dramatically, Eden continued her explanation, 'To ensure your heart is pure and the stone only passes to those with good intent, I have a test for you that you must complete before I hand it over.'

She gestured over to the scattered glass jars on her desk. 'The stone is hidden within one of these jars. You must figure out which. But be warned, some of the contents may not be what they seem, and most will be dangerous to impure hearts,' she added with a melodramatic flourish, throwing the back of her hand up to her forehead. She stepped back from the desk, giving the friends room to examine the collection of jars in front of them.

'Each one of them contains something that is bright orange or yellow,' noted Marta.

'Any one of them could contain the stone then,' added Eli.

'But we all have pure hearts, right?' countered Darcy optimistically. 'So whatever is in them shouldn't be dangerous to us.'

'It's a good point,' agreed Bella. 'Then perhaps we should all choose a jar we like the look of and open it to see what's inside?'

The friends agreed, each taking their time to carefully pick a jar. Marta selected hers first, lifting up the dainty yellow glass pot and delicately opening lid to see what was inside. She took a sniff of the contents and burst into uncontrollable laughter.

'Buttercup paste,' explained Eden. 'Don't worry, the effect will only last for a couple of minutes. Who will go next?'

'I will,' said Eli bravely. He held up his jar, unsuccessfully trying to examine what was inside through the glass. After a moment, he lifted the lid. Once again, the effect of the contents was instant. His bottom lip began to tremble and before long, huge floods of tears sprung from his eyes, puddling on the floor below. 'Gloom Pollen,' he said knowingly. He'd read about the effects of this in one of his botany books. While annoying and awful to witness, he was relieved that the side-effects were not toxic and would also only be temporary. Eden nodded, impressed.

Felix seized his jar next, snatching it boldly off the table and taking off the lid. He was unsure what to expect, but also impatient to get it over with. As soon as the scent hit his nose, a spasm ran through his body like electricity, growing into more uncontrollable movement until he found himself spontaneously gyrating around the room as if his limbs had a mind of their own. Marta, who had now finally stopped laughing, reassured him, 'Don't worry Felix, it's only Dancing Daffodil Stems, you'll be fine in a minute or two.' Felix nodded in acknowledgement while trying to regain control of his body.

By the time Eli and Felix had also returned to normal, the others were crowded round the dressing table again trying to decide which of the remaining pots to open. Bella was now growing tired of Eden's ridiculous games. She impatiently grabbed the pot closest to her and opened the lid. 'Wish me luck.' She grimaced. The thick oozing liquid inside had a familiar smell. Bella drank the contents, recognising the sweet taste of hyacinth honey immediately. 'Phew,' she said. 'There's just honey in this one, nothing to worry about.'

Eden smiled. 'Yes, that one is just to add to my tea before showtime. I did warn you I'm a trickster.' Bella rolled her eyes in response, getting increasingly bored of Eden's immaturity.

'But that does leave us with a bit of a dilemma,' Marta added, staring at the only two remaining pots on the table. 'So far, the contents of each jar has only had mild effects, which means it is likely one of these could be more dangerous.'

Darcy gingerly hovered her hand over the first pot, hoping for some kind of sign if it contained the gemstone or something more sinister. When no clarity came to her, she moved her hand over the other jar instead.

'Darcy, your necklace,' shouted Bella.

Noticing the sudden and urgent glow of the Protection Stone, Artemis swiped the glass jar from the table with her wing. It fell to the floor, shattering into tiny fragments of glass. A plume of yellow smoke rose ominously in the shape of a skull and crossbones from where the jar had fallen. Eli instantly recognised the acrid and unpleasant smell. 'Foxglove poison,' he stated bluntly and unimpressed. 'That is poisonous, even to humans.'

Darcy turned to Artemis, full of relief and gratitude. 'Thank you so much. You saved my life.' The noble hawk squawked a short reply and bowed her head in return.

'That must mean the stone is in the final jar,' predicted Darcy.

Keen to leave Pixie Hollow, she wasted no time opening the last pot and emptying the contents in her hand. As expected, a large orangey-yellow stone sat in her palm, shining with all the brilliance of the sun. The colour reminded her of Marta and her endless positivity, so she passed it to her for safe keeping. Marta tucked it safely in her cloak, hoping she wouldn't have to use it. She knew the stone would enable her to shape shift; but at the cost of a memory, she wondered if the price would be too steep.

'We've played your game now, Eden,' said Bella protectively and still irritated from their close call with the foxglove poison. 'It's time for us to leave.'

'That's fair enough, friends, venture on your quest,' she granted, shrugging off Bella's curtness. 'But you must come back again soon for a matinée. We do a mean performance of *Midsummer Night's Dream*,' Eden added with a slightly deranged chuckle. 'After all, who do you think encouraged Shakespeare to write about us fairies in the first place?' She winked.

Chapter Twenty-Five

Back outside Pixie Hollow, the friends regrouped to plan their next steps. They hadn't much liked Eden and her juvenile tricks, and the atmosphere within her lair had been stuffy and bizarre. Relieved to finally be back outside, they took a minute to enjoy the fresh air, savouring the moment of tranquillity.

'This will all change if we can't forge the Celestial Wand,' said Marta sadly, glancing around at the bright chlorophyll-coloured field. 'The magic will run out and then everything will begin to fade, just like the toadstool.'

It was an oddly pessimistic comment for Marta. Eli couldn't help but wonder if the burden of carrying the magical stone might already be affecting her. He smiled gently at his sister. 'Well, enough of that doom and gloom. Before we can think about combining the stones, we better get on and get the last one – the Peace Stone. You know where we have to go, don't you?'

'You're right,' Marta replied, shaking off her temporary spell of negativity. 'C'mon, everyone, it's time to visit Windwhisper Grotto. We must speak with Aelfric.'

Artemis beckoned the queen's giant pet buzzards with a loud and authoritative shriek. They met the friends promptly, bowing down dutifully so they could climb aboard. With two strong flaps of their lengthy wings, the buzzards took flight once again, gliding gracefully just below the clouds.

This time, Eli and Marta took the lead, knowing their way by heart back to their elvish town. Skilfully reading the landscape below, Eli instructed his buzzard to follow the sweeping curves of the river away from the Great Lake. The wake of buzzards followed, changing course to match. They soared on for what seemed like hours, crossing directly over the vast canopy of tree tops that made up the enchanted forest below, heading for another far corner of the realm. As they passed overhead, Marta waved covertly, hoping that Neptune would be in the forest below thinking of her too.

When they finally reached the edge of the mysterious woodland, the land opened to reveal a charming small village, centred around a bustling square. Even from their viewpoint, the friends could clearly see the town was alive with activity. A lively local market crowded the cobbled terracotta streets, lined with brightly coloured flags and bunting. Smoke rose from nearby chimneys, filling the sky with smells of freshly baked baguettes and decadent cakes; while shouts of street vendors could be heard echoing across the town with promises of fresh fruit and vegetables. The general noise and hustle and bustle was punctuated by the occasional clang of metal from the famous elvish farriers, crafting their esteemed and intricate horse shoes for lucky unicorns. As the friends passed overhead, the curious yet welcoming townsfolk pointed and waved.

'It's good to be home,' smiled Eli as they darted over rows of multi-coloured, unevenly shaped houses.

Marta agreed. 'It's the best, but we better hope Ma and Pa don't see us flying around up here instead of at the academy, or the realm running out of magic will be the least of our worries.'

Darcy felt a sudden pang of homesickness at the mention of home and parents. It was the first time she had felt that way since arriving in the realm and she pushed the feeling down, hoping it would stay there.

Now clear of the main square and surrounding houses, the friends could see a wide river running beside the town. After several bends, it eventually converged into a large and gently rippling crystal pool at the base of a great and old willow tree. The buzzards landed gently on a neighbouring bank, dodging clusters of tall water reeds so the friends could easily climb down from their necks.

'Elves like us love being close nature, so this really was the most perfect place to build the Elder's house. Welcome to Windwhisper Grotto,' explained Marta.

Concealed by the base of the giant tree and framed by long braids of leaves that rustled gently in the breeze, it was clear to see how Windwhisper Grotto got its name. The house itself had been built into and around the ancient willow tree so delicately that it looked like it had always been there. The friends approached the treehouse, huddling in front of the small arched doorway.

The door boasted a small but beautiful triangular stained-glass window depicting a sunset by the river, with a heron perched on a grassy bank in its centre. Eli squinted through the glass pane, trying his best to see if Aelfric was inside. Without much luck, he decided it would be best to knock and pulled down on the heavy bronze bell chain that dangled by the side of the door. An unusual melody chimed out to signal their arrival, and after a moment, footsteps approached.

As the door creaked open, the friends were greeted by a tall male figure with a familiar slant to his cheeks and point-tipped ears. He wore a deep grey cloak with white embroidered trim that blended into his long, white hair and contrasted against his striking silver eyes. The friends recognised Aelfric instantly from the last time they saw him at the wish wielding competition. A noble and gracious Elder, full of wisdom from his centuries of experience as a leader of the realm. He opened the door wide and welcomed them warmly into his home as if he had always known them.

'Eli, my boy.' Aelfric patted him firmly on the back as he walked through the door, thrusting him into the middle of the cosy cottage kitchen. Marta followed closely behind, making a more elegant entrance. 'Always a pleasure to see you too, Marta,' Aelfric nodded.

'And you must be Felix, of the famous Thunderbolts,' he added next, giving Felix a strong handshake.

Artemis, Bella and Darcy entered last, slightly more cautiously than the others. Aelfric bent from his waist into a deep and respectful bow, greeting Bella and Darcy more specifically. 'In all my long years, I never thought I would see the day when a pair like you both would arrive to fulfil our elvish prophecy. Warmest welcome to my humble home.'

A teapot whistled from the stove behind. 'Please help yourselves to iced buns from the table top. I'll bring some tea over,' Aelfric added.

The friends settled round the large oak kitchen table, content with full bellies and steaming mugs of nettle tea. It was almost as if Aelfric knew exactly what they needed before they realised it themselves. Bella wondered if he was already using the Peace Stone to read their thoughts. She eyed him with suspicion. Perhaps he made a habit of it.

Catching her eye, Aelfric smiled. 'You're right, Bella. Very perceptive of you.' He pulled out a twisted silver chain from under his cloak. A whitish-grey stone hung glowing at the bottom. 'It's been very useful over the centuries for maintaining peace in our land. I'm sure you can see why. But my hearing is definitely not what it used to be. And besides, it must now serve a greater purpose.' Removing the chain from his neck, he placed it over Eli's head. 'It now belongs to you, Eli. Use it wisely,' he added sagely.

Eli felt a swell of pride in his chest. It was a great honour to be the guardian of the stone, and in particular to have been entrusted it by their elvish Elder himself, whom his family had idolised for as long as he could remember. Although the stone itself didn't weigh much, the weight of the responsibility that came with it certainly did. Eli slid the chain safely under his tunic as Marta beamed at him proudly from across the table.

'Now to the business at hand,' began Aelfric. 'I'm sure by now you will have all heard the basics of the prophecy?' he asked rhetorically. 'Since the Great Goblin War, if the time ever comes that our realm is ever in danger, as it is now, a fairy godmother and special human with an unbreakable bond will arrive to save our realm. Together, they will have the power to combine the five precious gemstones to create the all-powerful Celestial Wand, bringing fresh magic, peace and hope to our realm and beyond,' he summarised, taking a big slurp from his mug.

'Yes, we've heard the stories Elder Albion,' answered Bella politely. 'But now that we have the stones, what do we actually need to do? Where do we even begin?' she asked restlessly.

'A wise question, Bella. With an answer that our elvish Elders have kept secret for centuries, so that should it ever be needed, we could entrust it into the right hands,' he answered solemnly. 'The wand must be created in a very specific place in our realm, the source of our Great Lake that nourishes our land.'

'Mount Imperial?' asked Felix.

'Yes,' Aelfric replied, 'you must travel to the very peak of the mountain to complete the ritual, and when you arrive, you must find the nest of a phoenix.'

The friends gasped, suddenly looking even more intimated. They knew phoenixes to be honourable birds, but also fiercely aggressive and territorial.

'A phoenix!' blurted Darcy. 'That sounds terrifying.'

Aelfric continued, trying to reassure them. 'This phoenix was born from the flames of the Great War and I personally reared her. Phoenixes are noble birds and ancient symbols of immortality, eternity and resurrection, so our Elders thought it would be the perfect creature to guard the sacred place where the stones must be combined to create the Celestial Wand. She will be protective of her nest, but tolerant of those with a pure heart,' he explained.

'Okay,' replied Bella, feeling slightly more at ease with his answer. 'But when we have found the phoenix, what must we do next?'

'All will become clear when you have found her nest,' answered Aelfric, cryptically, 'but I warn you, it is likely to require some kind of sacrifice.'

Darcy once again looked petrified. 'A sacrifice?' she burst out. 'What do you mean Elder Albion? I would never hurt anyone.'

Aelfric patted her hand gently, trying to soothe her. He didn't need the power of the Peace Stone to understand how overwhelming this must be for a human.

'Of course not, my dear,' he comforted her. 'I don't mean that kind of sacrifice, but you will have to give up something meaningful to you.'

'Oh,' Darcy exhaled sharply, relieved to hear. 'Well, if it helps to restore fairy magic, I'm sure it will be worth the cost,' she added resiliently.

Darcy was not the first human Aelfric had ever encountered, but in this particular moment, she was the most important. Because of her unique bloodline and connection with Bella, she held the key to creating the Celestial Wand. Although she didn't yet know the true significance of her heritage, they could not complete the ritual without her. The realm needed her help. And Aelfric needed her to play her part.

'You are remarkable, my dear,' Aelfric flattered. 'We are lucky to have you.'

'Elder Albion, one final question…' interrupted Bella. 'When we have created the Celestial Wand, how will we know that magic has been restored?'

Aelfric considered her question for a moment. 'You will notice a difference straightaway as fresh magic begins flowing from the river source at Mount Imperial down into the realm below. The land will seem healthier and colours will look more vivid again, but the true restoration will not be complete until a final spell has been performed on our toadstool,' he confirmed. 'As soon as you have the wand, you must bring it back to the toadstool where the Council and I will be waiting. We will take over from there by casting the spell needed to permanently restore magic throughout our land,' Aelfric advised.

The friends nodded in understanding.

'Now that you know what you must do, time is of the essence,' Aelfric rallied. 'There are many people in this land who would want the power of the Celestial Wand for themselves if they knew it was more than just legend, so you must be quick and discreet. Do not trust anyone you see on your journey and stop for no one,' he warned. He walked over to the kitchen counter and pulled out a small weathered scroll that had been hidden behind a mismatched rack of cookery books. 'Take this elvish map too,' Aelfric handed the scroll to Eli. 'It is the only one in existence and will direct you safely to the nest at Mount Imperial.'

'Thank you, Aelfric,' smiled Bella. She turned to her friends round the table. 'We know what we've got to do. Let's go and save our realm.'

Chapter Twenty-Six

Following Aelfric's magical map, the friends made light work navigating away from the elvish town towards Mount Imperial. As they left, the brightly coloured houses faded further into the distance and Eli and Marta waved down to their Ma and Pa somewhere below. They hoped to be able to return to the quaint elvish market town one day soon, with their parents still none the wiser about their adventure.

Across the other side of the river, the land was vast and sparsely populated. Scarce from a few small villages scattered across the landscape in small oasis-like pockets, the terrain was rough and dry, not unlike the goblin territory by the ancient magic mine. They soared onwards, taking turns to lead at the front following the magical map. As they did so, the others slept peacefully, snuggled up warm in the buzzards' feathery necks.

After a few hours' flying, the sun's golden rays began to tease the horizon. Eli was now at the lead of the pack and called back to the others to wake them. 'Time to wake up now, sleepy heads. We'll be there soon.' With a few long stretches and wide yawns, the friends awoke to a glorious sunrise. It felt much like the calmness before an imminent storm.

'That is breathtaking,' admired Darcy, staring wide-eyed at the orange and gold flecks of sunlight tickling the horizon. 'It's the most incredible sunrise I've ever seen.'

'Take it all in, Darcy,' replied Eli. 'Soon we'll need to climb higher to land on the mountain and this will all be concealed by clouds,' he added, gesturing to the magnificent view.

Sure enough as Eli had predicted, the buzzards soon changed course. They climbed steeply towards the thick cloud line ahead that looked like softly whipped ice cream. Darcy wondered if it would taste just as sweet as they passed through. She poked out her tongue to check as they breached bumpily through the clouds, disappointed to only taste water vapour. Fortunately, her dismay was short-lived. It was promptly replaced by awe at the staggering sight of a huge mountain up ahead that was growing closer by the second.

'That's Mount Imperial,' explained Eli, pointing towards the snow covered cap. 'The buzzards won't be able to get us all the way to the summit, so they'll have to land us on a ledge as close as they can to the top.'

As the buzzards drew closer to the mountain, they circled the rocky landscape until they could see a ledge that was big enough to land on. Following Artemis' signal, they narrowed in towards a large platform approximately three quarters of the way up the mountain. It wasn't as close to the summit as the friends would have liked, but at least it was flat and well sheltered. As they landed, they could see it offered a relatively safe and easy-to-climb path up to the top of Mount Imperial. Artemis had no doubt chosen this spot on purpose. They were lucky to have her as their guide.

'Okay, everyone,' instructed Bella when they had safely landed and dismounted their buzzards. 'It's only a short climb up from here, so leave anything you don't need behind and let's get to it.' Staying wrapped in their thick winter cloaks, they left their rucksacks in a pile to collect on their return. The temperature was much colder up in the mountain so they didn't want to wait too long before starting their climb. The air was also much thinner at altitude. Although this didn't affect fairies, Bella knew it might not be as easy for Darcy. She turned to check on her, worrying instantly at her pale complexion and raspy breath.

'I'm okay, Bella, don't worry,' panted Darcy. 'It's just a bit harder for me to breathe up here, but I'll be fine in a minute.'

'Okay,' Bella replied gently, not fully believing she was all right. She turned to the others. 'On second thought, let's take five minutes to rest and catch our breath before we climb.' They huddled round to keep warm and before long, drifted off into a gentle doze.

'Get up,' an authoritative voice from somewhere nearby ordered them awake.

The friends jolted awake in shock and jumped up to confront the intruder. They were stunned to see who had joined them unexpectedly on the ledge. A vaguely familiar white-cloaked figure, with olive skin, dark hair and white irises approached them. It was final-year student and highly skilled wish wielder, Mirabel Dawn. The friends were rendered temporarily speechless, unsure whether to be impressed, intimidated, or both. Eli considered it for a second. Definitely, both.

'I'm only here for the gemstones,' explained Mirabel with cool detachment. 'Hand them over and no one has to get hurt.'

Mirabel knew her fearsome reputation preceded her. She stood confidently in front of them with an outstretched hand, waiting for the first-year students to comply. She expected it would be a simple task to retrieve the stones. After all, a few first-year students and a human were no match for her and they were in way over their heads. This would be over quickly, she thought. She would soon be back in the comfort of her home.

Bella stood directly in front of Mirabel, matching her confidence with hands on her hips. 'You can't have the stones,' she said defiantly. 'We need them to create the Celestial Wand and restore magic to the realm.'

'You know about the Celestial Wand?' Mirabel asked with an edge of surprise to her stern voice.

'Yes.' This time Marta replied. 'Our Elder, Aelfric, told us everything. He would never lie to us,' she asserted confidently.

'I am surprised the Council told you about the Celestial Wand,' Mirabel conceded. 'I haven't found honesty to be a particular strength of theirs over the years,' she added earnestly, shaking her head. 'But regardless, that really doesn't change anything. It is my duty to stop this and I can't let you combine those stones.'

'You can't stop us,' shouted Darcy in response. She was unsure if it was wise to provoke Mirabel further, but also beyond caring. They had come too far now not to succeed.

Mirabel paused, weighing up the situation, while Darcy, Marta, Eli, Felix and Artemis flanked Bella's sides in a display of loyalty and collective strength. They might have been far less experienced than Mirabel, but they sure weren't going to make this easy for her.

Mirabel didn't want to hurt anyone if it could be avoided, but she also knew she would have to if they didn't give in. Her lifelong duty depended on it. She tried reasoning with them one last time instead. 'Think about it,' she urged them. 'Did Aelfric really tell you everything about the wand? Do you know what it is truly capable of? Do you even know what it will be used for?' she asked them persuasively in quick succession. 'I mean, sure, you'll be saving the realm in the short term, but do you even know at what cost?'

The friends were quiet, pondering the sudden seed of doubt that had been planted in their minds. They had been so trusting of the Fairy Council that they hadn't thought to ask any of those questions. Mirabel sensed she was finally getting somewhere. 'Why don't you leave it to fairies like me who know what we're doing?' She added her final plea, 'This is the last time I'll ask nicely. Give me the stones.'

Bella remembered Aelfric's guidance and banished any doubt from her mind. She knew Mirabel was trying to manipulate them and wasn't going to fall for any more tricks.

'We said no,' she replied audaciously and definitively.

Mirabel shook her head in disbelief. She had tried everything she could think of to prevent a battle, but now felt that she had no choice. She raised her wand in preparation to fire.

Sensing imminent danger, Darcy's gemstone necklace began flashing with urgent pulses of turquoise light and her protective shield changed once again from wood to solid platinum. On Bella's instruction, she hid behind it, hoping to avoid the incoming blasts of elemental magic.

The unusual display momentarily confused Mirabel, distracting her just enough for her first strike to fly wide. The bright sizzling laser of magic narrowly missed Bella's chest, instead carving a smoking zigzag into the rock behind.

Bella was equal parts outraged at the attack and relieved it had missed. She turned urgently to her friends. 'We have to use the stones and we have to use them now,' she ordered. She knew it was unlikely Mirabel would miss again and next time they might not be so lucky. Above all, she had to protect Darcy. It was now or never if they were going to escape.

Fuelled with anger, Bella retaliated first. She clutched the Heart Stone, channelling its magic towards

Mirabel. She hoped its power would trick Mirabel into thinking she didn't want to hurt them. From the flash of confusion that crossed Mirabel's face and the way she briefly lowered her wand, Bella could only assume the trick was working.

'Who's next?' she asked her friends.

Marta raised her hand, clutching tightly onto the sunshine-yellow Shapeshifting Stone. She wished deeply to change their form for a moment into something small and less easy to hit. The timing was perfect. Just as Mirabel fired her next shot, the friends shape-shifted into small multi-coloured butterflies, completely avoiding the attack yet again. They sprung back to their original form like a bubble bursting its own illusion. But for Marta, something was now missing. She thought it might have something to do with Neptune. Or perhaps something to do with flying unicorns. But she couldn't quite put her finger on it. The curse of the stone had taken away a sliver of unknown memory. Stolen from her mind like a piece of a jigsaw puzzle, leaving behind a vaguely accurate, but frustratingly incomplete picture.

By now Mirabel was visibly aggravated. Staring back at the smouldering rubble where her last strikes had landed, she raised her wand again. Felix seized his opportunity before she had another chance to fire. He took hold of his Realm Jumping Stone and grabbed Eli's hand, encouraging his friends to form a chain. Just like he had been taught in class, he took a deep breath and envisioned them all at the top of the mountain. With a sudden jolt, that's where they were. Suddenly at the summit. Suddenly safe. It seemed almost too simple.

'That was amazing, Felix,' praised Bella, dusting herself down.

'Quick thinking, pal,' added Eli, giving him a fist bump.

Even Darcy seemed to be smiling. She was in much better shape after this realm jump.

'Thanks,' Felix beamed back.

But although they knew where they were, the curse of the Realm Jumping Stone meant they couldn't be sure when. Alerted by a faint rustling of snow from the ledge below, they carefully peered over the edge of the summit to investigate. Felix pulled them back silently. On this occasion, it looked like they had only jumped back in time several minutes. Mirabel had only just made it onto the ledge below.

'Phew,' exhaled Marta.

'We won't have long before she figures it out though,' whispered Bella as they quickly hid back out of sight. 'Let's get a move on and find our phoenix.'

Chapter Twenty-Seven

The summit of Mount Imperial was covered in a dense layer of shimmering white snow, blanketing the ground like a thick coating of royal icing piped onto a freshly baked birthday cake. Staring over the edge of the mountain into the surrounding abyss, there was little to see of interest. The view this high up was shrouded by sweeping billows of cloud that seemed to stretch on for miles in every direction. The air was also damp and uncomfortably cold. The friends pulled their cloaks up high around their necks, bracing themselves from the frost.

Darcy felt momentarily confused. Everything about this environment seemed surreal to her. A perfect contradiction to where she would expect to find a smouldering phoenix, with its bright red plumage and association with fire. She supposed that at least the phoenix would be easy enough to find on the summit. It couldn't have strayed far on such a narrow mountaintop.

As the friends started to explore the summit, it became obvious that Darcy's prediction was accurate. The closer they got to the centre of the mountaintop, the thinner the carpet of snow became. Following the signs of warmth, the friends were guided towards the middle of the mountainous platform, where the now just-crisp layer of sparkling frost melted into complete nothingness, leaving behind a large ring of exposed rock at the peak.

In the centre of the ring was exactly what the friends had been hoping to find. A large and glorious phoenix. The gigantic eagle-like creature looked magnificent, with bright ruby-red plumage and long wing feathers that blazed with shades of gold and garnet. It had a sharp amber beak and gleaming talons that made it look equally astonishing and fearsome. Eli knew these creatures could live for hundreds of years and this phoenix certainly looked mature and formidable. Whatever they had to do to create the Celestial Wand would be difficult with this creature on guard. Fortunately for the friends, the phoenix sat sleeping within a giant nest of interwoven sticks and branches, oblivious to their presence. That is until Darcy took a step closer to the nest.

'Darcy, wait,' called Bella.

But it was already too late. Hearing the scuff of gravel nearby, the phoenix's bright auburn eyes shot open to see the unexpected visitors. Alarmed at what it saw, the phoenix squawked and flapped its wings aggressively, trying to fend off the intruders. The strong gust of wind knocked Darcy backwards, forcing her to grab onto a nearby rock to stay upright. She didn't know which was worse. The impending cliff edge or her current proximity to the enraged phoenix. Yet, despite these dangers, Darcy's gemstone pendant refused to flash. It was unusual behaviour for her Protection Stone, and it left her well and truly puzzled.

As the phoenix stood to attack again, it revealed a large golden egg concealed within the centre of its fortified nest. Being the closest to the nest, Darcy was able to make out several intricate symbols that had been delicately carved into its golden shell.

'The egg has the symbols for the five gemstones scrawled across it,' Darcy called back to the others. 'Remember, the ones from the queen's library book?'

Bella nodded. 'That must be why it's getting so agitated,' she added, 'it must be guarding the egg because it's the key to creating the wand.'

'Regardless,' grumbled Felix, 'there's no way we're getting close enough to the egg if we can't get this bird under control.'

'You're right,' chimed in Marta. 'Think, everyone. There must be something we can do to distract it.'

'We might not need to,' replied Eli. 'I have an idea.'

Eli knew what he must do. Aelfric had told him to use the Peace Stone wisely and that's exactly what he intended. He lifted the silver chain that held the luminous white stone from out of his cloak and held it up for the phoenix to see. With his friends waiting patiently by, Eli closed his eyes and focussed on the phoenix in front of him, trying his hardest to hear its thoughts and emotions. To his friends around him, it already seemed to be working. The phoenix began to calm, visibly relaxing its wings and closing its eyes, while the Peace Stone softly glowed in Eli's hand. After a few minutes of unspoken dialogue between Eli and the phoenix, they both opened their eyes once more, seemingly in mutual agreement.

'The phoenix was just frightened of having all of us around,' Eli began to explain to his friends. 'It doesn't want to hurt us.'

'That must be why my Protection Stone didn't flash this time,' suggested Darcy.

'I think you're right,' responded Eli calmly. He continued explaining what the phoenix had told him. 'The phoenix was put here long ago by the Fairy Council to guard the golden egg where the gemstones could be combined. It has been the phoenix's life's duty to protect the egg and prevent the unworthy from creating the Celestial Wand. The phoenix thinks we might be worthy to combine the gemstones, but before we can try, we must prove ourselves.'

'How do we do that? 'asked Bella cautiously.

'It's as Aelfric said,' advised Eli, 'we must all make some kind of sacrifice, giving up something precious to us to prove we are selfless enough to deserve the wand. We will then be able to open the golden egg and combine the gemstones.'

The friends nodded warily, as Eli stepped forward first, showing them what to do. He laid his magical elvish map at the phoenix's feet.

'This was a gift from one of my heroes, Aelfric Albion, which brought us here safely to your nest,' he explained to the phoenix. 'Please accept it as a gift.'

Felix followed next. He walked up to the giant bird and presented a packet of lavender cookies that had been hidden in his pocket. 'Take these. These cookies are my favourite treat, made to my mother's top-secret family recipe. I've only carried them with me this far because they make me feel close to home.' He bent down gloomily and placed them on the floor next to Eli's map.

Standing back in line next to Bella and Darcy, Marta suddenly gasped as the memory she had previously lost to the Shapeshifting Stone came back to her. In her mind's eye, she could clearly see herself on the back of a unicorn, giggling with Neptune and her friends as they swerved through the clouds. Everything about the memory was magical and she felt a sudden pang of guilt that she had temporarily forgotten it. She looked down at her Shape Shifting Stone. It was glowing hues of soft yellow, as if suggesting something to her. She knew what she must do. She marched over to the phoenix and looked it squarely in the eyes. 'Take that memory back,' she said. 'It is one of the most precious things I own.' She walked back to her friends with a tear in her eye, and the treasured memory was once again lost to the stone.

Watching Marta's pain brought a tear to Darcy's eyes too. She knew all too well what it was like to lose something precious, and she was about to have to do it again. By far the most valuable thing Darcy owned was her gemstone pendant. It had always made her feel closer to her mother. It had always protected her. And even when she hadn't realised it, it had always connected her to the magical realm. She walked up to the phoenix, holding up her turquoise gemstone necklace. 'I understand that sacrificing this may mean I can never come back here,' she acknowledged, 'but to save the magic in your realm and mine, and to ensure that fairy godmothers can continue to protect their humans for generations to come, I know it will be worth it.' With a final reluctant squeeze of the stone, she placed it on the floor at the feet of the phoenix.

It was then Bella's turn to make the final sacrifice. Watching the sadness of her friends, she knew in that moment that they were the most important things in the world to her. The thought of losing her bond with Darcy in particular felt heartbreaking, but she also knew it was a real possibility. Without the connection between the Protection Stone and the magical realm, Bella had no way of knowing if her magic alone would be strong enough to bring Darcy back through a dream cast ever again. She worried that they may not be able to see each other when this was all over, but she believed that fulfilling the prophecy was bigger than just them. It was the right thing to do. For the fairy realm and beyond. She approached the phoenix and laid down the strongest thing she could think of to symbolise her magical bond of friendship with Darcy. The small rose-gold pocket watch that she had originally found in her first dream casting lesson. The one that belonged to Darcy, connecting them from the moment they met.

The phoenix was visibly moved by their sacrifices and satisfied that they were worthy. It bowed to each of them in turn, giving its blessing. A small, blood-red tear trickled down its cheek onto the ground below, followed by a thin billow of smoke that rose in its place. It stared at Eli for a moment, communicating telepathically with him. Eli followed the phoenix's instructions and waded over to the centre of the nest to collect the golden egg. It was much heavier than it looked. He carried it slowly and awkwardly back to his friends and flicked the ornate latch to open its lid.

'We each have to put our stone into the five slots, as indicated by the symbols,' explained Eli, placing his Peace Stone in accordingly. Felix copied next, followed by Marta and Bella. Darcy picked up her stone and gave it one last squeeze to say goodbye. She placed it in the final slot and mournfully closed the lid. As Eli had been instructed, he laid the completed egg back at the feet of the phoenix and went back to join his friends in a line behind.

The phoenix looked content the ritual had been satisfied. It stared knowingly into each of their eyes one last time, as if seeing directly into their souls. With a final bow, the phoenix lowered its head to rest its amber beak on top of the golden egg. Within moments, the egg began to change colour, heating from gold, to brown, to bright white, before finally bursting with blinding light like a dying star. Suddenly, as if the egg could take it no longer, it exploded in front of them, shattering into billions of tiny fragments of glittering rainbow-coloured dust.

Shocked and confused by what they saw, the friends' mouths gaped open. They expected combining the stones to create something, not obliterate it. The wise phoenix squawked impatiently, sensing their frustration. It didn't need any translation from Eli this time. They kept watching the floor where the golden egg had just been. Slowly but surely, without any plausible explanation other than magic, the tiny fragments began to cluster, joining together again into new chucks of rainbow crystal. The clusters merged, resurrecting themselves until they eventually formed a beautiful crystal wand.

'We've done it,' exclaimed Bella triumphantly. 'That's the Celestial Wand!' She rushed over and swept it up from the floor in amazement, feeling a pulse of powerful energy run through her veins. It felt slightly unnerving, but also exciting. Holding it in her hands, it was suddenly clear why fairies like Mirabel might want the wand for themselves, but she didn't have long enough to ponder much further. She knew time was now of the essence to save their toadstool and restore magic to their realm. They had to get home.

Chapter Twenty-Eight

Making haste, Bella whistled for Artemis and their giant buzzards, who dutifully appeared from the ledge below, scooping the friends up onto their feathered necks. Within moments, they were once again soaring through clouds, racing away from Mount Imperial, back towards their precious toadstool in its emerald meadow. As they flew further into the distance, Bella glanced over her shoulder for a final time, relieved that Mirabel was still nowhere to be seen. She wasn't naive enough to think it would be the last they saw of her, but thankfully for now, their fight was over.

Just as Aelfric had promised, the realm was already looking revived as fresh magic began to seep through the land once more, spreading down from its source at the summit of Mount Imperial. As the friends glided across each new landscape, they couldn't help but smile as plants and flowers burst into new life around them, flooding the realm again with rich and vivid colours.

Flying at full speed and spurred on by their success, it didn't take them long to reach the meadow. They touched down victoriously in front of a large crowd of anxious onlookers. It was clear from their surprised expressions that the new magic had not yet reached the centre of the realm. The crowd stared on mournfully at the deflated and now sagging toadstool. It looked brown and weak. They really didn't have much time.

Bella and her friends rushed to the centre of the meadow, where the queen and members of the Fairy Council had congregated. They were surrounded by their worried classmates, and more concerningly, their Principal, Loretta Featherstone. The friends hadn't seen their principal since they secretly fled the academy, trying to find a way to get Darcy home after inadvertently bringing her through to their realm in the first place. They had no doubt she would be severely disappointed with them. They just hoped she wasn't angry enough to consider expulsion.

Bearing a mixture of relief and frustration, Loretta Featherstone rushed over to greet them, her deep orange cloak flowing behind. Her translucent silver skin looked ever thinner than usual, more like tissue paper, and judging by her deep crimson curly hair, she had been under considerable stress. She was flanked by her receptionist, Belinda Nightingale, who strutted behind in a teal dress, trying to keep pace, while brandishing a thick clipboard.

'As you can imagine, I am infuriated with the bunch of you,' Loretta called out angrily, before softening her tone. 'But most importantly, I am so glad you're all okay. I have been worried sick at the thought of losing some of my students.' Her shoulders slumped as she exhaled sharply like a deflating balloon.

'Fortunately, as a favour to me, our queen told me everything, but that does not excuse your behaviour. I am still INCREDIBLY disappointed in you for sneaking off and putting yourselves in such danger. Not to mention putting the life of a human at risk.' She turned to smile apologetically at Darcy, before facing the others again with new-found frustration. 'Honestly, it makes my hair red just thinking about it.' She shivered. 'So, when we are done here today, enjoy your last evening of freedom, because when you get back to the academy you are going to be in detention for the foreseeable future. Do I make myself clear?'

'What?' spluttered Eli, flabbergasted yet hopeful. 'Does that mean we're not expelled?'

'At least not on this occasion,' Principal Featherstone exhaled, before softening her voice again. 'I can't go losing my best students, now can I?'

The friends beamed in response, but Principal Featherstone was reluctant to let them off too lightly.

She added with final authority, 'Just don't let it happen again.'

Eagerly interrupting the reunion, the queen pushed past her guards to join Principal Featherstone. She was dressed in a resplendent cream-and-lilac dress, adorned with a moonstone tiara. 'I hope you haven't been too hard on them, Loretta,' the queen mock scolded the principal with a knowing smile. She was well aware Loretta wouldn't have punished her favourite students too much. Besides, with any luck, they had completed their mission and were about to save the realm. The queen turned warmly to Bella and Darcy. 'Do you have the Celestial Wand?'

'We do,' answered Darcy, as Bella offered it over.

The queen was ecstatic. She seized the wand, savouring the power of raw, untapped magic coursing through her. 'You have no doubt gone through many trials and tribulations to get this wand and have put yourself in great danger for the sake of our realm,' she declared earnestly to the group of friends. 'Thank you.' Looking out over her sea of subjects, she called out to them. 'Thanks to the heroic efforts of these friends,' she gestured to Darcy, Bella, Marta, Eli and Felix, 'it is now time to cure our toadstool and restore magic to our land.'

The growing mass of fairies cheered in anticipation as the queen raised the Celestial Wand high above her head and took aim at the drooping toadstool. With a swish and flourish, intertwined strands of rainbow-coloured magic shot forth from the wand, slamming into the toadstool with full force. It stood unwavering, absorbing every ounce of pure power until it could take no more, slowly expanding like a giant sponge. When fully replenished, the now plump toadstool erupted into spectacular colour, shooting out spores in every direction. They landed delicately, scattering themselves across the full expanse of the emerald meadow, sprouting up into hundreds of tiny magical toadstools. The crowd rejoiced.

Surrounded by a backdrop of loud cheers, Bella turned to the queen. Something had been niggling her since their encounter with Mirabel and feeling the effects of the wand for herself. 'What will happen to the Celestial Wand now, Your Majesty?' she asked inquisitively.

The queen sensed her doubts but was eager to brush them away. 'Nothing for you to worry about, Bella. It will be stored safely in my royal vault, under the care of the Fairy Council,' the queen dismissed her concerns. 'Besides, now is a time for celebration.'

A small bell rang in the back of Bella's mind, reminding her of something Mirabel had said back on the ledge. She ignored the thought for now, pushing down the small intrigue that played in her mind and instead allowing herself to be swept up again in the atmosphere of celebration.

Their classmates swarmed around them merrily. Neptune rushed over to Marta, sweeping her up off the floor into a big hug. 'You did it Marta, you all saved the realm!' He smiled at her with pride, gently placing her back down on the ground to momentarily release her from his strong arms. Marta could no longer deny she had a full-blown crush. She stretched onto her tip toes to give Neptune a deliberate peck on the lips. Blushing and speechless, he could do nothing except grin back soppily at her. His younger sisters, Tempest and Talia Summersong, watched on swooning.

On the other side of the group, Finn, Gale and Jupiter greeted Felix like a hero. They rallied round him like a celebrity, enthusiastically patting him on the back.

'Well done, mate,' praised Finn, giving him a fist bump.

To Eli's surprise, even Scarlett and Stella looked impressed. Scarlett breezily sauntered over to him. 'You know, Eli, I was pretty sceptical about elves before meeting you.' She paused straight-faced, before continuing, 'But you might just change my mind.' Without waiting for any kind of response, she strolled off just as casually as she had appeared, back to join Stella, Gale and the other boys. Eli was shocked and frozen on the spot, which amused Marta greatly. She threw her little brother a wink.

Standing separately, a short way off from others, Bella turned to Darcy and gave her a big hug. 'I suppose this means you'll have to go home now, Darcy,' she said sadly. 'I'll miss not having you here.'

'I'll miss you too, Bella,' she smiled fondly. 'You will come and visit me in my dreams though, won't you?'

'Of course,' chuckled Bella. 'I'll be there to watch over you in the human realm too, just as soon as I've graduated. You won't keep me away.'

'Good,' Darcy laughed. 'But in the meantime, thank you for everything, Bella.' It was clear she wanted to say more, but didn't quite know where to begin. She paused thoughtfully.

'What is it, Darcy?' Bella gave her a gently nudge. 'You know you can tell me anything.'

Darcy smiled. 'It's just that before I met you, I spent so much time alone, missing my mother and wishing I could find somewhere I belong.' Darcy's eyes glistened with a mixture of sadness and hope. 'But now I realise, just by being here, just by meeting you, my wish has come true.'

So moved by what she had overheard, the queen couldn't help but interject. 'You know, if my beloved parents have taught me anything, it's that friendships like yours are rare to find, and when you do, they are something to treasure and hold onto.' She reached up to her tiara and pulled out something small that had been concealed within. It was a delicate golden key, embellished with a teardrop-shaped moonstone, with a small hole on top so it could be threaded onto a pendant. She placed it in Darcy's palm, closing Darcy's hand on top. 'Darcy, our realm owes you a great debt. It might not ever be repaid, but I hope this is a start. Take this enchanted key. It might not be able to replace the gemstone you lost from your mother, but it will enable you to come and go from our realm as you please. All you have to do is use it in your dreams.'

Darcy was blown away by the queen's generosity. 'Thank you, Your Majesty,' she squealed back excitedly. Overjoyed, Bella and Darcy re-joined the rest of their friends. By now, the music was in full swing and the party was well underway. The atmosphere felt light, surrounded by carefree fairies dancing and jiving cheerfully around the meadow. The friends huddled together, totally content, savouring the moment as they watched the realm celebrate into sunset. Although it had taken them the best part of a realm-rescuing adventure to realise it, they had everything they needed right there. Because, as it turned out, in a realm full of wishes, the real magic was right in front of them all along.

The adventure continues…

Secrets of the Roseblade Society

by Bianca Rodriguez Jacobs

Chapter One

As a hush of sleep finally descended over the magical realm, a gentle calmness washed over the snoozing towns with a tender kiss of moonlight. But not everyone rested. Lurking in the darkest corner of the realm was a growing rumble of resentment and bitterness. Increasing in power and hungry for revenge.

Somewhere in the gloom hid a mysterious figure. Far from the comforting caress of moonlight and lit only by the warmth of an enchanted candle, the shadow scrawled manically onto a single page of parchment. An ominous warning, scratched into the fibres with ink the colour of spite. So acidic that it sizzled onto the paper with a hiss, burning its threat like venom and filling the air with the smell of bile.

Determined to end their letter just as dramatically, the mysterious figure finished with a flourish. Five words were scraped tauntingly into the parchment, each oozing with more malice than the one before until they almost tore through the paper below:

I HAVE THE CELESTIAL WAND.

The mysterious shadow sat back and laughed, admiring their work. It was a deep foreboding sound, bordering on psychotic, that fortunately there was no one else around to hear. Finally content, they rolled up the parchment into a small, unassuming scroll and clipped it onto the scrawny leg of an imprisoned messenger hawk. In the last few hours before sunrise, the eager bird launched free from its shadowy den, unknowingly carrying its menacing message towards the centre of the realm.

As the sun peaked tenderly over the horizon, the rest of the realm began to rise. Sleepy yawns escaped through open windows, as slowly but surely, the fairy world became alive with activity once more. Fairy folk throughout the land whistled merrily as they began their morning routines. With typical good cheer, they filled up on hearty breakfasts of cinnamon buns and honey cake, blissfully unaware of the evil that lurked in the shadows.

The royal castle was no exception. Hidden behind its imposing sugarplum-coloured turrets, preparations are well underway for the day ahead. Not unlike the rest of her subjects, the queen awoke to the delicious smell of sweet pastries. The irresistible scent meandered seductively up to her chambers, beckoning her down to breakfast in her favourite room of the whole castle, the library. The opulent library was like a greenhouse, bursting with a varied mix of tropical plants and flowers that cocooned the room in an oasis of vivid colours. As a maid poured her usual morning beverage, the queen took her seat on a plush purple throne in the centre of the room, next to a flamingo-shaped fountain that bubbled gently into a small pool below. As she did every morning, the queen admired the incredible architecture of her palace while sipping contently at her steaming mug of candied-lemon tea. The peaceful silence punctuated only by the occasional clink of china or clank of silverware as servants rushed to replenish the morning's feast. Everything was as it should be.

'Letter for you, my queen,' proclaimed a pretty, olive-skinned maid, with tight dark curls and white irises. She presented a small scroll on top of an intricate silver platter.

The queen appraised the fairy, graciously looking her up and down. With so many staff in the palace, the queen was ashamed to say she didn't know all of her servants by name. It would truly have been an impossible job. But although the queen couldn't place this particular fairy, she did have an air of familiarity about her. The queen took the scroll with a curt smile and unravelled it greedily, eager to absorb its contents.

As the queen read, all colour drained from her face. 'Check the vault,' she ordered, shouting abruptly to her nearby royal guard. She had believed her royal vault to be impenetrable. The safest place to store the all-powerful Celestial Wand to prevent it from falling into the wrong hands now the realm was once again safe. She hoped the letter was just a hoax. A cruel scam full of lies. Her mind raced and her heart pounded.

The answer came moments later. It was not the outcome she had wished for.

'The wand is missing, Your Majesty,' her guard replied gravely, shaking his head.

In a state of shock and disbelief, the teacup slid from her lap and shattered onto the floor, sending tiny fragments of fine bone china scattering in all directions like marbles. A great rage rose within her that felt like fire coursing through her veins.

'It must be those "Roseblade Society" bandits,' she seethed to herself. 'They've always wanted to control the realm. They must want the wand for themselves.'

The queen paced anxiously across the room, trying to understand how such a disaster could have happened. She knew the stakes were higher than ever, for whoever held the wand, held the power to control the realm. If the Celestial Wand was in the wrong hands, their world as they know it could be destroyed. And the human one was in danger too.

'I must find it,' she fumed, filled with equal parts fire and determination. 'I must protect the realm from those thieves.'

Hearing the news, the pretty maid scurried from the room, eager to avoid the queen's temper. She had a secret of her own to keep, and she had somewhere else she needed to be. She left the castle as quickly and discreetly as she could, travelling with great purpose as the queen's shrieks faded into the distance.

Acknowledgements

When I started writing this story, I could have only imagined my scribbled notes would one day become the novel you are reading today. At the time, it all seemed like a ridiculous dream, so I am beyond grateful for the support of those around me who have helped me to bring this story to life. You really are my own personal fairy godmothers, thank you!

To my friends, thank you for encouraging me to be brave and take a chance. You continue to inspire some of my favourite characters with your endless grace and good humour. I hope you like what you've read, and I hope I've done you proud.

To my family, I dedicate this book to you. Without your unwavering belief in me, this novel would have never happened. Mum and Dad, thank you for your ongoing encouragement and for always teaching me to work hard and dream big. Bella, you are, as always, a continued source of inspiration with your boundless 'main character energy'. Thank you for being my sister and my biggest cheerleader. CJ, there is no word count long enough to explain how grateful I am for all your love and support. Thank you for your endless encouragement, infinite puns, and for never letting me get hangry. I really could not have achieved this without you.

Last, but not least, thank you to you, my readers. While it still feels a bit surreal to be holding a real-life copy of my debut novel, it gives me so much joy to know that you are right here with me. Thank you for believing in the magic and coming along on this adventure. There's plenty more to come.

About the author

Bianca Rodriguez Jacobs lives in Wiltshire with her husband, where she enjoys long walks in the countryside, balanced with plenty of delicious home-cooked food.

Growing up with a lively younger sister, Bianca always enjoyed creating magical worlds for them to play in, which has carried into her love of fantasy stories set in faraway lands. She is also very proud of her half-Spanish heritage, often using it to inspire Latin characters in her stories that reflect the richness of our diverse society.

After studying Psychology at the University of Bristol, Bianca's passion for writing led her into the world of internal communications, where she has worked for several years until realising there simply isn't enough magic involved in the corporate world.

When she isn't writing, Bianca enjoys nothing more than coaching her local girls' football team, spending time with family, and an occasional glass of Aperol Spritz.

BRJACOBS_BOOKS

Follow Bianca on Instagram @BRJacobs_Books.